D0467380

REC'D

WHAT SUCCESSFUL PEOPLE KNOW ABOUT LEADERSHIP

Books by Dr. John C. Maxwell
Can Teach You How to Be a REAL Success

Relationships

25 Ways to Win with People
Becoming a Person of Influence
Encouragement Changes Everything
Ethics 101
Everyone Communicates, Few Connect
The Power of Partnership
Relationships 101
Winning with People

Equipping

The 15 Invaluable Laws of Growth
The 17 Essential Qualities of a Team Player
The 17 Indisputable Laws of Teamwork
Developing the Leaders Around You
Equipping 101
How Successful People Grow
Intentional Living
JumpStart Your Growth
Learning from the Giants
Make Today Count
Mentoring 101
My Dream Map
Partners in Prayer
Put Your Dream to the Test
Running with the Giants
Talent Is Never Enough
Today Matters
Wisdom from Women in the Bible
Your Road Map for Success

Attitude

Attitude 101
The Difference Maker
Failing Forward
How Successful People Think
How Successful People Win
JumpStart Your Thinking
Sometimes You Win, Sometimes You Learn
Success 101
Thinking for a Change
The Winning Attitude

Leadership

The 21 Irrefutable Laws of Leadership, 10th Anniversary Edition
The 21 Indispensable Qualities of a Leader
The 21 Most Powerful Minutes in a Leader's Day
The 360 Degree Leader
Developing the Leader Within You
The 5 Levels of Leadership
Go for Gold
Good Leaders Ask Great Questions
How Successful People Lead
JumpStart Your Leadership
Leadership 101
Leadership Gold
Leadership Promises for Every Day

WHAT

SUCCESSFUL PEOPLE
KNOW ABOUT

LEADERSHIP

ADVICE FROM AMERICA'S #1
LEADERSHIP AUTHORITY

JOHN C. MAXWELL

**CENTER
STREET**

NEW YORK   BOSTON   NASHVILLE

Center Street
Hachette Book Group
1290 Avenue of the Americas
New York, NY 10104
centerstreet.com
twitter.com/centerstreet

Originally published as *Good Leaders Ask Great Questions* by Center Street, 2014

First Edition: May 2016

Center Street is a division of Hachette Book Group, Inc.
The Center Street name and logo are trademarks of Hachette Book Group, Inc.

The publisher is not responsible for websites (or their content) that are not owned by the
publisher.

The Hachette Speakers Bureau provides a wide range of authors for speaking events. To find
out more, go to www.HachetteSpeakersBureau.com or call
(866) 376-6591.

Library of Congress Cataloging-in-Publication Data

Names: Maxwell, John C., 1947– author.
Title: What successful people know about leadership : advice from America's
    #1 leadership authority / John C. Maxwell.
Description: First Edition. | New York : Center Street, 2016. | Series:
    Successful people | Includes bibliographical references.
Identifiers: LCCN 2015049881| ISBN 9781455548125 (hardback) | ISBN
    9781478924340 (audio cd) | ISBN 9781478924333 (audio download) | ISBN
    9781455548118 (ebook)
Subjects: LCSH: Leadership. | Employee motivation. | Interpersonal relations.
    | BISAC: BUSINESS & ECONOMICS / Leadership. | BUSINESS & ECONOMICS /
    Management. | BUSINESS & ECONOMICS / Motivational. | BUSINESS & ECONOMICS
    / Office Management. | BUSINESS & ECONOMICS / Skills.
Classification: LCC HD57.7 .M394289 2016 | DDC 658.4/092—dc23 LC record available at
http://lccn.loc.gov/2015049881

ISBN 978-1-4555-4812-5 (hardcover), 978-1-4555-4811-8 (ebook)

Printed in the United States of America

WOR

10 9 8 7 6 5 4 3 2 1

This book is dedicated to Collin Sewell. Every month for two years I answered a great question you sent me. As I mentored you from afar, I watched you grow from a good to a great leader. Now I enjoy mentoring you personally and am delighted to count you as a friend.

Contents

Acknowledgments

Thank you to:

Charlie Wetzel, my writer;

Stephanie Wetzel, for editing the early manuscript and
managing my social media;

Audrey Moralez, for her research assistance;

Carolyn Kokinda, for typing the first draft; and

Linda Eggers, my executive assistant.

Introduction

I chose my career path at age eighteen, earned my degree, and went to work. That first job gave me a leadership position. But it didn't make me a leader. I worked in that position for three years and I thought I was successful. However, it wasn't until I was in my next position that I realized how little I knew about leadership. I discovered that I was a hard worker, but not much of a leader.

That's when I started asking myself, "What do successful people know about leadership that I don't?" That was the start of my lifelong leadership journey. I started reading books to help me become a better leader. I started paying attention to how successful people in my field led. And I started asking questions—lots of questions. In fact, I've often told the story of how I researched who the top ten leaders were in my profession, contacted them, and offered them what was a large amount of money to me for thirty minutes of their time.

Many said no. Some said yes, and gave me exactly thirty minutes. Others graciously gave me even more of their time and refused to take the money I offered.

I learned a lot from those leaders—and from many others. More than forty years have passed since those meetings, but I continue to learn as much as I can about leadership.

Today, some people call me an expert, though I still consider myself a student. And nearly every day, others are asking me questions about leadership. I'm glad to share what I've learned so far. And that's what I'm doing in this book—sharing insights on leadership that I've gleaned through personal experience and observing successful people.

Whether you're a brand new student of leadership, as I was fifty years ago, or a seasoned veteran, I believe you will find useful insights in these pages that will help you to lead others better or to mentor other leaders. The chapters were prompted by questions people have asked me, and teach some of the essentials for successful leadership:

1. How to Lead Yourself
2. How Leadership Works
3. How to Get Started in Leadership
4. How to Resolve Conflicts and Lead Challenging People
5. How to Succeed Working Under Poor Leadership
6. How to Navigate Leadership Transitions
7. How to Develop Leaders

You can read the book from front to back, tackling the progressively difficult subjects, or you can go straight to the topic that will help you most right now. This book is designed to meet you wherever you are on the leadership journey.

I wish you great success, and encourage you to pass on to others what you're learning.

WHAT SUCCESSFUL PEOPLE KNOW ABOUT LEADERSHIP

1

How to Lead Yourself

When I conduct Q and A sessions with leaders, the vast majority of questions I receive are about self-leadership. Why? I think many people understand intuitively that if you can't lead yourself effectively, everything else in your life will be a struggle.

Self-leadership comes first. It makes every other kind of leadership possible. It's where personal credibility is established.

As you read through this chapter, I encourage you to think about how well you lead yourself—even if you are a seasoned high-level leader. Some of the challenges you face may come from the way you lead yourself. You may attribute them to someone or something else, when you actually need to look at yourself as the source. As you'll see from the first topic, no one is immune to this problem.

Why Does Leading Myself Seem More Difficult than Leading Others?

One of the reasons we have such difficulty leading ourselves is that we have blind spots preventing us from seeing where we have problems and fall short. These are areas in which people continually fail to see themselves or their situation realistically. Everybody has some; few people recognize their own. We see those of others more clearly. Why? Because we see ourselves by our intentions. That often gives us a false impression of who we are or what we do. We give ourselves the benefit of the doubt because we put things into context. On the other hand, we see others in light of their actions. For that reason we seem to be more objective when judging them.

While blind spots cause all people problems, they can be especially harmful in leaders. Because leaders influence others and their actions affect a team's, department's, or organization's outcomes, the problems that come from their blind spots are exaggerated. Their blind spots have a multiplying effect on the people in their sphere of influence.

To lead yourself successfully, you must identify your blind spots and deal with them effectively. To help you do that, I want to talk about the four most common and destructive blind spots among leaders:

1. A Singular Perspective

Having too singular a perspective might be a problem for you if ...

- No matter how a conversation begins, you end up talking about your favorite subject.
- You keep giving the same speech, lecture, or piece of advice over and over again.
- You are always right, even though nobody is always right—on any subject.

Instead of viewing everything from such a singular perspective, effective leaders make an effort to see things from different points of view.

2. Insecurity

Insecure leaders continually think of themselves first. They worry about what others think of them. They fear that they may look weak or foolish or insignificant. Insecure leaders take more from people than they give. Because they feel they are less, they seek validation more. Insecure leaders also limit their best people. They have a difficult time seeing others rise, because it threatens them. And they cannot genuinely celebrate the victories won by others, because they are often jealous. Giving others their due makes them feel like less.

Because insecurity is often hidden in a blind spot, leaders often don't recognize it in themselves. How do you know if insecurity is a problem for you? Answer the following questions:

- Do you feel you *need* credit or have a hard time giving credit to others?
- Do you keep information from your staff to protect your position?
- Do you try to keep your staff away from good leaders, because you're afraid they may be stolen?
- Are you threatened by the growth of others?
- Do you often micromanage others or feel you deserve the credit for your team's accomplishments?

In the end, insecure leaders limit their people and their organization.

3. An Out-of-Control Ego

Another major blind-spot area for leaders is ego. Egotistical leaders believe they know it all. They believe others are inferior to them. And they often think the rules don't apply to them.

Egotistical leaders are usually rigid and closed-minded. They are out of touch with their clients and employees, they blame others when anything goes wrong, and they live in a state of denial. Their only positive quality is that they don't talk about others—because they never think about anyone but themselves.

How can you tell if you're an egotistical leader? Answer the following questions:

- Do you think you're indispensable or that no one else can do a job as well as you can?
- Do you believe others are always to blame when things go wrong?
- Do you disregard the ideas of others or feel others' ideas are inferior to yours?
- Do you feel superior, or do other people often feel put down by you?

Egotistical leaders don't look for input or answers from anyone other than themselves.

4. Weak Character

When you ask most people what it takes to be successful, they list talent, opportunity, and hard work as the primary ingredients. While those things are essential, so is character. Why? Character protects your talent. With character, all those other attributes help a leader to be successful. Lack of character is a deal-breaker when it comes to leading yourself or others. Character is the sum total of all our everyday choices. It is putting right values into action every day. It's consistency of values, ideals, thoughts, words, and actions.

If you suspect that character weaknesses may be holding you back, note your answers to these questions:

- Do you often miss deadlines?
- Do you make vows, resolutions, or decisions to change and then go back to your old behavior?
- Do you place more importance on pleasing others than you do on maintaining the values you espouse?
- Are you willing to shave or shade the truth in order to get out of a tough spot?
- Do you do what's easiest, even when you know it's not what's best?
- Do others show reluctance to trust you?

If you answer yes to any of these questions, there may be areas of your character that need some work.

How to Overcome Your Blind Spots

1. **Assume that you have blind spots.** If you don't believe that you have blind spots, that *is* your blind spot!

2. **Ask those who know you best to identify your blind spots.** If they are honest, they will tell you what you aren't seeing about yourself.

3. **Assume your blind spots cannot be removed by you alone.** Everyone needs help seeing and dealing with blind spots. Don't think you can deal with yours on your own.

4. **Openly discuss your blind spots with your inner circle.** Be open with the people who care about you and want to help you.

5. **Develop and empower a team to cover your blind spots.** You may eventually be able to overcome many of your blind spots. Until then, make sure your team prevents them from derailing you or the team.

When values, thoughts, feelings, and actions are in alignment, people become focused and their characters are strengthened. That allows leaders to lead themselves successfully.

What Gives a Leader Sustainability?

Leadership isn't easy. Every day, leaders must wake up and lead themselves before they lead anyone else. Because other people are depending on them, they must keep the fire burning within themselves. They must know where they're going, know why they're going, and help others get there. To stay energized and on course, leaders can sustain themselves by tapping into four areas:

1. Passion

Passion gives you two vital leadership characteristics: energy and credibility. When you love what you do and do what you love, others find it inspiring. How many people do you know who became successful at something they hate?

2. Principles

Successful leaders stay true to their principles—to their beliefs, gifts, and personality. They don't try to lead in a style that does not suit who they are. They can honestly state, "My leadership style is comfortable and reflects who I truly am." The better you know yourself and the more true you are to yourself, the greater your potential for sustainable success.

3. Practices

Nearly anyone can achieve flash-in-the-pan success. We all get lucky from time to time. But if we want to sustain success—as an individual or a leader—we need to implement right and regular practices that help us to do the right thing day after day. Successful people do daily what unsuccessful people do occasionally.

4. People

The people around you will either wind you up or wear you down. Ideally everyone would lead a great team, have fantastic friends, maintain a strong inner circle, and possess a loving family. Many leaders don't have all these. If that's the case for you, don't be discouraged. Even if you have only one person in your corner cheering you on, you can still lead successfully.

I believe that no leader ever needs to burn out. Just remember to tap into your passion, stay true to your principles, implement the right practices, and surround yourself with the right people.

What Are the Most Important Values for a Leader?

All individuals have to decide what values they will embrace, what they will live for, what they would die for. Those values come from their core beliefs and their faith. I won't address those here, because I believe you must wrestle them down personally. Instead I'll talk about the *leadership* values that I believe are most important.

Servanthood: Leading Well Means Serving Others

If you want to lead others but you are unwilling to serve people, I think you need to check your motives. If you are willing to embrace servanthood, not only will you become a better leader, you will help your team, help the people your team serves, and make the world a better place.

Purpose: Let Your *Why* Direct Your *What*

Success comes from knowing your purpose in life, growing to your maximum potential, and sowing seeds to benefit others. If you miss any one of those three things, I don't think you can be genuinely successful. I also know that you cannot achieve the second and third parts fully without first discovering the first. You can't grow to your potential if you don't know your purpose.

Integrity: Live the Life Before You Lead Others

Great teams are made up of people with diverse skills. But when it comes to values, habits, disciplines, and attitudes, there needs to be unity. That starts with the example set by the leaders. If the leaders are undisciplined, the people will follow suit. When you become a leader, you must focus more on your responsibilities than on your rights. You must raise your standards. You must do more than you expect of others. If you live the life first and lead well, others will respect you. And the chances are good that they will be willing to follow you.

Relationships: Walk Slowly Through the Crowd

Leadership impact is drawn not from position or title but from authentic relationships. Treat people with kindness and respect, and go to where they are to connect with them. A lot of leaders assume that people will come to them if they need or want something. But effective leaders initiate. They communicate vision. They seek out opportunities. They start initiatives that will benefit the organization.

They know that they will never possess what they are unwilling to pursue. They want good relationships with the people who work with them, so they seek those people out. They ask them questions. They learn who they are. They offer assistance. They find ways for them to succeed. If you want to become a better leader, become highly relational.

Renewal: Replenish Yourself Daily

Life is demanding. People are demanding. The more you lead and the more you succeed, the more others will expect from you. If you don't make an effort to replenish your energy, feed your soul, and renew your mind, you will run out of gas. Replenishing yourself requires your attention. You have to be intentional about it.

Certainly there are other important values for leaders, but these are the ones I put at the top of my list. I encourage you to examine your own core beliefs and decide which values are most important to you.

What Is the Most Effective Daily Habit for Any Leader to Develop?

If you could cultivate only one habit to practice every day of your life, I believe it should be this: giving more than you receive. I say that because having a giving mind-set has so many benefits:

Giving Acknowledges That Others Have Helped Us

No one succeeds in life on his or her own. Every one of us has been helped along the way by other people. When we give to others, we acknowledge that by paying it forward.

Giving Requires Us to Get Beyond Ourselves

When your mind-set is to give more than you take, it forces you to think of others more than of yourself. You have to pay attention to others and what they want. You have to figure out how to give it to them. These things shift your focus from yourself to others. That very fact makes you less selfish.

Giving Is by Nature Intentional

People rarely give by accident. They must make an effort to give. It is an act of will. That intentionality grows us and makes us more proactive—important qualities for leaders.

Giving Changes the World—One Person at a Time

What would the world be like if everyone tried to give more than he or she took? People would change. It's difficult for a healthy person to keep receiving from others without giving something back. Out of abundance comes generosity. Give generously to others without the hope of return, and the person receiving is changed and wants to pass it on. Once you have the mind-set of giving, the more you receive, the more you want to give. It becomes a positive cycle. As it spreads, not only do individuals change, but so do communities.

Three Questions to Ask Before You Can Effectively Give More

1. **What have you been given?** Even people from the least advantaged backgrounds have positive experiences to draw upon.

2. **What do you have?** Discover what talents, skills, and passions reside in you that you can pass along to others.

3. **What can you do?** What opportunities do you currently see to add value to others?

How Does One Change One's Heart to Increase the Desire to Add Value to and Serve Others?

You can't be an effective leader by keeping people at arm's length. You can't mentor them if you aren't close to them. You can't add value if you don't know what they value. And they won't ever go the extra mile for a leader who doesn't care about them.

Changing your heart toward people is a choice. You must *decide* to love people and be authentic and vulnerable with them. You must choose to let them into your life so that you can add value to them and they can add value to you.

I believe that such a decision will lead to many more

wins than losses, both personally and professionally. Once you've been part of a team in which people give not just their minds but also their hearts, you won't ever want to go back. You'll always want to be open with people.

If I Am Reaching Goals and Achieving Success, Why Should I Take Care of Developing Myself as a Leader?

If you want to be a leader, you need to keep growing. What got you to where you are today will not get you to where you want to go tomorrow. You must grow into your tomorrows. The choice is yours whether or not you will.

Do you want to be ready for the next opportunity when it comes? When it arrives, it will be too late to prepare. The time to get ready is now.

You don't know what life will throw at you. You will face tragedies and opportunities. How do you know you will be ready for them? Grow today.

Requirements of a Plan for Growth

Growth does not just happen on its own. You have to be intentional about it. If you want to grow, plan to grow. Here are the things you'll need to do:

1. Set aside time to grow.
2. Determine your areas of growth.

3. Find resources in your areas of growth.

4. Apply what you learn daily.

How Do You Lead with Humility When in the Tough Corporate World It's Viewed as a Weakness?

Humility doesn't mean being weak. It just means thinking of yourself less. It means being realistic and grounded. It means valuing others and their contributions. People like working with a leader with those characteristics. Humility encourages team building, values teachability, opens us up to feedback, allows us to face reality and our mistakes, promotes character building, and enlarges our potential. If you pair excellence with humility, people not only won't run over you, they will respect you.

How Transparent Should a Leader Be?

As a leader, you should not hide bad news. People always find out. Of course, there are times not to be totally candid with people. For example, if you have a family member whose privacy needs to be protected, you need to honor that. But in general, people appreciate transparency. It allows them to connect. And it can inspire them.

However, you also need to ask yourself why you're telling the bad news. Are you doing it for the good of the team? Are you communicating to connect with your people and to encourage them? Or are you doing it because you are hoping people will pick you up? If it's the latter, that's not a good reason. If you're going through a personal crisis, it's OK to let people know that you may not be yourself right now, but that it'll only be for a season. And then carry on. You don't want to wear your people out with your personal challenges.

How Can I Overcome the Loneliness I Sometimes Feel as a Leader?

First of all, let me point out that there's a difference between aloneness and loneliness. I sometimes crave aloneness— to think, create, and hear from God. I like to take time to think and reflect. I enjoy that time. Aloneness fills me up. I meet it with a sense of anticipation.

Loneliness is altogether different. Leaders often have to go first. That can be lonely. There are weights that leaders need to carry. There are messages that they must be the ones to communicate. There are critical decisions they must make. In a well-led organization, 90 percent of decisions are made by the people close to the problems—at the level of implementation. The other 10 percent are tough decisions that must be made by a leader.

When I have to make a tough decision, I share it with people in my inner circle. That helps greatly. The other thing you can do is let loneliness drive you to aloneness. When you are feeling the weight of leadership, find ways to get by yourself and think things through.

How Can Leaders Develop the Ability to "Filter" Their Emotions to Make Good Leadership Decisions?

One of the most important principles of decision making for leaders is not to make decisions at an emotional low point. When you're in an emotional valley, your perspective isn't good. Everything looks difficult. Having said that, I acknowledge that there are times when you *must* make leadership decisions during emotionally difficult times. To help you in such circumstances, here is what I advise:

1. Do Your Homework

The first defense against having unfiltered emotions negatively affect your decision making is to consider the facts. Define the issue. Put it in writing if needed. Then gather information, considering the credibility of your sources. The more solid information you have, the better you can fight irrational emotions.

2. List Your Options and Where They Could Lead

Another part of the fact-finding process is to think about outcomes. Brainstorm every option you can think of and what the potential results could be. This will help you root out ideas that feel good emotionally but aren't strong rationally.

3. Seek Advice from the Right People

There are two kinds of people you need to consult. The first group includes the people necessary to make a decision happen. If they aren't on board, you will be in trouble if you make the decision. The second consists of people with success in the area of consideration who have your interests at heart. They can give you good advice.

4. Listen to Your Instincts

You don't want your emotions to run away with you when you're making decisions, but you also don't want to ignore your instincts. Often your instincts warn you in a way that goes beyond the facts.

5. Make Decisions Based on Principles and Values You Believe In

When all is said and done, you must be able to live with the decisions you make. Be sure they align with your values, and you can live them out.

Leading yourself is perhaps the least discussed yet most important aspect of leadership. What happens when leaders fail to do the right things internally, day in and day out? They get into trouble. The news is littered with the names of people with great talent and huge opportunities who did wrong things and cultivated bad habits when others weren't looking.

   If you and I want to be successful in life, successful in leadership, and successful in finishing well, we must learn to lead ourselves successfully.

2

How Leadership Works

Leadership is a complex subject. I'm sixty-nine years old and I'm still learning. I intend to be a student of leadership until the day I die. But I will never lose sight of the truth that leadership starts with influence and builds from there. Please keep that in mind as you read this chapter.

Does Everyone Have the Potential to Be an Effective Leader?

Everyone has the potential to lead on some level, and anyone can become better at leading. While it is true that some people are born with traits that help them to become better leaders than others, those natural traits are only the beginning. Great leaders don't start out great. Leadership is developed, not discovered. It's a process. Three main components come into play in the development of a leader:

Environment: Incarnation of Leadership

A person's environment has a tremendous impact on him or her. Leadership is more caught than taught. If you grew up in a leadership environment, you probably recognized your own leadership ability early. If you're in a positive leadership environment now, you are probably having leadership qualities encouraged in you, and they may be starting to come out. The right environment always makes learning easier.

If you're not in a leadership environment now, and have never spent time in one, you may be having difficulty knowing what it means to lead. If so, you will need to find a positive leadership environment to help you in your leadership development. Is it possible to learn leadership without a conducive environment? Yes, but it's difficult, and your development will be slow.

What Does a Growth Environment Look Like?

Others are *Ahead* of me.

I am continually *Challenged*.

My focus is *Forward*.

The atmosphere is *Affirming*.

I am often out of my *Comfort Zone.*

I wake up *Excited.*

Failure is not my *Enemy.*

Others are *Growing.*

People desire *Change.*

Growth is *Modeled* and *Expected.*

Exposure: Inspiration for Leadership

One of the things I find most inspiring is exposure to great leaders. I love to hear great leaders speak. I get ideas from reading their books. I enjoy asking them questions. I get fired up watching them lead. I am even inspired by getting to visit their work spaces. I've also visited every presidential library. When my wife Margaret and I visit a library, we spend an entire day just soaking in leadership and being inspired by it.

Where Will You Go for Leadership Inspiration?

Whom do you admire as leaders? Plan to go hear someone you admire speak. Take a trip to a presidential library or a museum. Make an appointment to interview an impactful leader. Get inspired!

Equipping: Intention for Leadership

The one thing you can do to have the greatest impact on your leadership potential is to be intentional every day about becoming equipped to lead. Every book you read, every lesson you absorb, every principle you apply helps you to become a better leader and takes you another step forward in your leadership potential.

Leadership is influence, and it can be learned. You can learn to connect with people. You can learn how to communicate. You can learn to plan and strategize. You can learn to prioritize. You can learn how to get people to work together. You can learn how to train and equip people. You can learn to inspire and motivate others. Most leadership skills can be taught to people; people can be equipped to lead.

What Is Your Plan for Leadership Growth?

If you do not have a plan, the odds are against your growing as a leader. Set some goals and develop a personal strategy to grow in the coming year. Then break down the plan into daily and weekly disciplines.

How Can You Be a Leader if You're at the Bottom?

The good news is that you can be a leader no matter where you are. You don't need a title. You don't need a position. You don't need a formal education. All you need to begin is the desire to lead and the willingness to learn. The key is influence.

Leadership Is Influence

Your ability to influence others will be the single greatest factor in your success as a leader. Influence is an invitation anyone can make to another person.

Influencing Others Is a Choice

We can be indifferent to people, pursue our own agendas, have bad attitudes, and refuse to work with a team. Or we can care about people, be inclusive, work to be positive, cooperate with others, and try to positively influence them. Every day it is our choice. If we choose to try to influence people, we can lead from anywhere.

Our Influence Is Not Equal in All Areas

Just because you have influence with someone doesn't mean you have influence with everyone. Influence must develop with each individual. The most effective leaders are intentional about trying to influence others positively. And they understand that they have to work to increase their influence with individual people.

With Influence Comes Responsibility

In our culture, people tend to focus on their rights. People who desire to lead often seek leadership positions because of the perks and privileges. However, as leaders we should always be aware that leadership carries responsibility, that what we do affects the people whose feelings and well-being are within our influence. The influence we have with others will be positive or negative. We choose which one it will be.

People of Positive Influence Add Value to Others

Groundbreaking Major League Baseball player Jackie Robinson observed, "A life isn't significant except for its impact upon other lives." If you choose to influence others and become a better leader, I hope you will do so to add value to others.

What Is the Ultimate Purpose of Leadership?

First and foremost, leadership is about adding value to people. If you want to be successful as a leader, you need to make others better. You need to help them remove self-imposed limitations and encourage them to reach their potential. You can do that by doing the following:

Listen to Their Story and Ask Questions

You don't really understand people until you hear their life story. If you know their stories, you grasp their history, their hurts, their hopes and aspirations. You put yourself in their shoes. And just by virtue of listening and remembering what's important to them, you communicate that you care and desire to add value.

Make Their Agendas Your Priority

Too many leaders think that leadership is all about themselves. Good leaders focus on the needs and wants of their people, and as far as it is within their power, they make their people's hopes and dreams a priority. There is great power when the vision of the organization and the dreams of its people come into alignment, and everybody wins.

Believe in Them

If you want to help people, believe in them. When people believe in themselves, they perform better. That's why I say it's wonderful when the people believe in the leader, but it's more wonderful when the leader believes in the people. To increase people's belief in themselves, express your belief in them. In general, people rise to the level of your expectations. If you see the value in everyone and let them know that you value them, it helps them, it helps the organization, and it helps you as a leader.

Discuss Ways to Accomplish Their Visions and Create Plans That Fit Them

When you know what makes people tick and you understand their hopes and dreams, you have the potential to add value to them in a powerful way. Talk to them about ways to help them accomplish their vision while they do their work and help the organization. Then, together, formulate a plan to help them do it.

Help Them Until the Vision Is Accomplished

It's one thing to say you want to help people on your team. It's another to actually follow through and assist them all along the way. When you follow through, you not only help them, you also build your leadership credibility and your influence, not only with them, but with everyone on the team.

There is no downside to adding value to people. Yes, it will cost you time and effort. But when you add value to people, you help them and make them more valuable. If you're a leader, when your people are on purpose and content, you help your team. When your team is more effective, you help your organization, because it becomes better. And the whole process will bring you a deep sense of satisfaction.

What Is the Difference Between Delegating and Abdicating Responsibility?

When leaders hand off tasks to others, they typically do it in one of two ways: they delegate tasks or they dump them.

People who abdicate responsibility neglect leadership when they dump tasks on other people. Good leaders always take into account the skills, abilities, and interests of the person doing the work. Dumping usually happens on the spur of the moment. It ignores the person's need for more information or training. Dumping often occurs when people in authority want to get rid of a problem or remove an unpleasant task from their plate.

In contrast, good delegation includes carefully selecting the right person for a task. Good leaders take into account the skills and abilities best suited to complete the task at hand. Leaders who delegate well establish what the goals are, grant the authority to get the job done, and supply the necessary resources for the job, yet encourage independent action on the part of the person doing the work. In the end the leader who delegates the job is still responsible for seeing that the job gets done.

What Is the Greatest Challenge in Answering the Call to Leadership?

The greatest challenge in leadership is making decisions that affect other people. It's hard to make good decisions every day for people. But the fact that decision making can be difficult and painful doesn't let leaders off of the hook. They still need to make early and tough decisions, because leaders who decline to make decisions create insecurity among followers and undermine their own leadership.

If you want to become a better leader, become willing to make tough choices and uncomfortable decisions. Those may include the following:

Courageous Decisions: What Must Be Done

Hard-won progress often comes as the result of difficult decisions that can be scary. Sometimes the organization is on the line and the only people in a position to make the courageous calls are the leaders.

Priority Decisions: What Must Be Done First

It is the responsibility of leaders to look ahead, see the bigger picture, understand the greater vision, and make decisions based on the priorities of the whole team and organization.

Change Decisions: What Must Be Done Differently

One of the most difficult yet vital roles of leaders is to be change agents for the sake of the team and organization. Most people don't like change. They fear it and resist it. But leaders often provide the education and impetus for making changes.

Creative Decisions: What Might Be Possible

Sometimes making tough decisions calls for experience. But often what's really beneficial is creativity. Good leaders think outside the box and help the team break through barriers and cover new ground.

People Decisions: Who Should—and Should Not—Be Involved

The most difficult of all decisions often directly involve people. It's not always easy to find the right person for a given job. It's even more difficult to decide whether someone is no longer right for the team. In fact, this is such an important and complex process that I've dedicated chapter four to resolving conflict and leading challenging people.

Though decision making is difficult, it is vital to good leadership. H. W. Andrews asserted, "Not all of your decisions will be correct. None of us is perfect. But if you get into the habit of making decisions, experience will develop your judgment to a point where more and more of your decisions will be right." And as a result, you will become a better leader.

Can a Leader Actually Lead and Serve at the Same Time?

It is a common misconception that it's the role of followers to serve and of leaders to be served. That is a faulty view of good leadership. Most potential leaders overestimate the perks and underestimate the price of leadership. When they focus on the benefits of leadership, they become self-serving.

If you want to be the best leader you can possibly be, no matter how much or how little natural leadership talent you possess, you need to become a serving leader. And here's the good news: it's a choice. What it takes to serve others is within your control:

1. Serving Others Is an Attitude Issue

Leon A. Gorman of L.L. Bean observed, "Service is just a day-in, day-out, ongoing, never-ending, unremitting, perse-vering, compassionate type of activity." First and foremost, it's a matter of attitude. And it's contagious. If you serve your people well, and the members of your team in turn serve you well, it will further motivate you to serve them, creating a positive cycle.

2. Serving Others Is a Motives Issue

Robert K. Greenleaf, founder of the Robert K. Greenleaf Center for Servant Leadership, observed, "The servant-leader *is* servant first....It begins with the natural feeling that one wants to serve, to serve *first*." If you go into leader-ship with the motive to serve others, the team, and the orga-nization, it will be hard for you to go wrong.

3. Serving Others Is a Values Issue

If you value people, you will want to add value to them and serve them. Everything you will accomplish as a leader ultimately hinges on the people you work with. Without them your success as a leader will be greatly limited. Every day, organizations are responsible for the greatest waste in business—that of human potential. If you can develop people and help them discover their strength zones, everybody wins.

I believe there is no division between serving and leading. The foundation of effective leadership is actually service. People can tell what your attitude is. It shows in everything you do. Good leaders see their role as that of servant, facilitator, value adder, success-bringer—but they do this quietly, without fanfare.

Questions Leaders Should Ask About Serving

Are you a serving leader? To find out, ask yourself these questions:

1. Why do I want to lead others?
2. How important is status to me?
3. Do others work *for* me or *with* me?
4. Am I glad to serve others and do it cheerfully?
5. Is my team better because I am on it?
6. Exactly how is it better?

If you find it difficult or "beneath" you to serve others, your heart may not be right. To earn the right to lead in greater things, first learn to serve in smaller ones.

What Are the Top Skills Required to Lead People Through Sustained Difficult Times?

One of the most challenging tasks any leader faces is being a change agent and leading people through tough times. But it can also be one of the most rewarding. Tough times show us ourselves. The people we lead find out who they are. As leaders, we also find out what we're made of.

The best way to approach tough times is to try to see them as opportunities. Most people want their problems to be fixed without their having to face them, but that is an impossibility. As a leader, as a coach, as a catalyst for turnaround, you need to help people solve problems, take responsibility, and work to make things better. Most of the time, people need to dig themselves out of their difficulties—whether or not they were the cause of them. They need help, which you can give them in the form of advice, encouragement, and positive reinforcement, but everyone needs to do his or her part and work together.

With that context in mind, here is how I would recommend that you lead and serve people during difficult times:

1. Define Reality

Most people's reaction to tough times or a crisis is to say, "Let's forget the whole thing." So what is a leader to do?

Define reality for people. As the leader of a team, you need to help people define the things that are holding them back. Then you need to define the things that will free them up. People cannot make good choices if they don't know what these things are, and many have a hard time figuring them out on their own. You're there to help them.

2. Remind Them of the Big Picture

Leaders are keepers and communicators of the vision. They bear the responsibility for always seeing the big picture and helping their people to see it. People need to be reminded of why they are doing what they do, and of the benefits that await them as a reward for their hard work.

That doesn't mean that the vision is 100 percent clear to the leader, especially during difficult times. But that's OK. When I'm leading people through a difficult situation, I often don't know all the answers. But I know there *are* answers, and I will do everything I can to make sure we find out what they are. That gives people reassurance.

3. Help Them Develop a Plan

If you have helped people by defining reality and showing them the big picture, the next task is to identify the steps required to go from here to there. Not everyone finds it easy to do that. As a leader, you need to come alongside them and help them figure it out.

4. Help Them Make Good Choices

People's choices define who they are and determine where they go. It's true that we don't choose everything we get in life, but much of what we get comes from what we've chosen. As a leader, the more good choices you have made throughout your life, the better you have probably positioned yourself to help others, not only because you have gained experience and developed wisdom, but also because repeated good choices often lead to personal success and greater options. If these things are true for you, put them to good use by helping others navigate difficult waters.

5. Value and Promote Teamwork

When times get tough, everybody needs to work together if they want to get the team out of trouble. No team can win and keep winning unless everyone works together. It's the responsibility of leaders to promote teamwork and get team members cooperating and working together.

6. Give Them Hope

Hope is the foundation of change. If we continue to hold hope high, and we help others to do the same, there is always a chance to move forward and succeed. Crisis holds the opportunity to be reborn. Difficult times can discipline us to become stronger. Conflict can actually renew our chances of building better relationships. It's not always easy to remember these things. As leaders, our job is to remind people of the possibilities and to help them succeed.

Is It Possible to Be a Leader in All Areas of Your Life?

The short answer to this question is no. And here's why. You cannot develop influence with everyone. There isn't enough time in a day or enough days in a year. Developing influence is a process. So choose where you will invest yourself to develop influence and become an effective leader. The leadership skills you develop will help you in all areas of life, but you cannot expect to lead in every area of life. That simply isn't realistic.

What Are the Rhythms of Leadership as You Age?

The decades of life are not the same for everyone. We all know that. And there are both positives and negatives to every age. But you can look at the decades of a leader's life and make some generalizations about them:

- **Twenties—Alignment:** We build our foundation and prepare for future success.
- **Thirties—Adjustment:** We try different things and find out what works and what doesn't.

- **Forties—Advancement:** We focus on our strength zone and make the most of what works.
- **Fifties—Assessment:** We reevaluate our priorities and hopefully shift from success to significance.
- **Sixties—Ascendance:** We reach the top of our game and the height of our influence.

Of course, not everyone's life works out this way. That's why I believe it's more useful to think of our lives in terms of seasons. Every season has a beginning and an end. Our lives are not static. Even if a person chooses not to grow, life does not remain the same. (People who refuse to grow professionally, decline.) While we are in a season of life, we should do all we can at that time. Too often people give less than their best, thinking they can make it up later. What they don't understand is that once a season has ended, they often *can't* go back. They don't get another chance. When the new season comes, we need to be ready to make the appropriate changes to move on to it.

Another truth is that the seasons always come in sequence. Spring always follows winter. The same is true of the seasons of success. You cannot harvest life's rewards without first planting seeds. Yet many people want to spend their entire lives in the harvest season. It just doesn't happen.

Each of us is responsible for managing the seasons of

our own lives. We have all been given seeds. We all have to weather storms and drought. And it's up to us to plant and cultivate several "crops" for life simultaneously. We must recognize that we may be in one season of family life, a different season of spiritual life, and yet another of leadership life. We must do what's right for the season in each area, and do things in order, if we want to eventually see harvests in life.

Many people fail because they are out of sync with time and place in their seasons of life. When this happens they become frustrated and may begin to believe that it's impossible for them to achieve anything significant, and that leads to discouragement. I believe it is possible for all people to reap a rewarding harvest according to their ability, but they must learn the secret to mastering each of the four seasons:

Winter Is the Season for Planning

For unsuccessful people, winter is a time of hibernation, drudgery, and low expectations.

For successful people, winter is a time of beginnings. This is the time for vision and dreams. It is a time of anticipation. Goals are set and plans are made during winter. In any individual area of life where you're experiencing a winter, spend some time thinking about the harvest you hope to reap someday. Think big about what could be. Then plan how you will get there.

Identify Your "Crops" and Their Seasons

Which areas of life are important to you? These are the fields where you plant the "crops" for your life. Have you already identified them? If not, make a list.

Once you have identified the areas of life that are important to you, determine which season you are in for each. This will help you to work your way through each of the seasons. Remember, you will not be in the same season in every area.

Spring Is the Season for Planting

People who don't understand the seasons of life get spring fever. They continue to daydream when they need to be working.

Successful people have spring fervor. They understand that spring is the time to put winter plans and ideas into action. It's a time for enthusiastic activity. It takes energy, perseverance, and sacrifice. And it takes good timing. This is why people who get a head start in life are sometimes able to make such a great impact. If you've missed opportunities to plant in the past, don't keep waiting. Start moving! The sooner you plow and plant, the better your chance to see a good harvest.

Summer Is the Season for Perspiration

When you mention summer to most people, they think of vacation. But for the successful person, summer is the time for continual and regular cultivation, watering, and fertilization. It is a time of great growth.

In winter many people dream of success. Some realize that they must learn and grow to achieve their goals and live their dreams. Those people plant in spring by taking a tangible step toward growth: buying a book, finding a mentor, identifying a conference that will help them. But for many people, the effort stops there. They don't read the book, follow through with the advice of their mentor, or attend the conference, or they do but don't apply what they learn. They stop sweating through the hard, tedious, sometimes painful, but always productive work that summer requires.

Summer can be a taxing season. The days are long and there's more work that needs to be done than there are hours in the day. But successful people keep at it. They put in the effort—even though they can't really see that it's paying off. And that's how it often is when you're cultivating. You just have to keep working and trust that the plans you made in winter and the hard work you're doing now are going to pay off if you stick with them.

Autumn Is the Season for Produce

Just as watching trees lose their leaves can bring some people feelings of loss, some people realize only when it's too late that they should have made hay while the sun shone. However, to successful people who have made the most of each season, autumn is a time of reaping. It is the time when they receive the products of their labor. It brings feelings of accomplishment. There is no better season of life.

Your ultimate goal as a leader should be to work hard enough and strategically enough that you have more than enough to give and share with others. Maybe you didn't get to start as early as others did. That doesn't matter. Wherever you find yourself, do what's right for the season. Give it all you've got, and don't worry too much about the outcome. In time, if you understand the seasons and work with them, the harvest will come.

3

How to Get Started in Leadership

Some people have a clear vision for leadership. There is an organization they desire to create or a task they want to accomplish. They see something and they try to seize it. They start performing a service or creating a product, and if it's successful, they soon need help. When they hire their first employee, they start leading.

However, most people move into leadership differently. They find themselves in a situation where someone asks them to lead something—at work, in their community, or at church—and they agree to take on the responsibility. Or they help to give direction to a project or task because no one else is doing it, or because the person in charge is doing it so poorly that they worry it will fail. So they take charge and organize it themselves, hoping to see it succeed.

How you come into a leadership role matters less than

how you handle it. And the key question you need to ask yourself is, "Why do I want to lead?" If you want to help other people, your team, and your organization, you're starting off on the right foot. If your desire is to fulfill a worthy vision, one that will help people and make the world a better place, you're headed in the right direction. If you're doing it to add value to others and not just yourself, you are seeking to be a leader for the right reason. And it is your duty to become the best leader you can possibly be.

How Can a Young Leader Get Buy-in When He Doesn't Yet Have a Track Record of Success?

I've known a lot of young leaders who are very eager to share their vision and want to know why everyone doesn't immediately jump in to help them accomplish it. Until you have credibility, don't even try to get buy-in for your vision. You won't get it. You need to earn trust before people will buy in, and you must earn it through character and competence.

When you take on a new leadership position, how much temporary trust you receive will depend on many things. The culture of the organization. The credibility of your predecessor. The influence of the people who put you into place. If the environment and the culture are negative, people may assume that you won't be a good leader and give you very little grace. In a more positive environment, people may be open to you and willing to give you the benefit of the doubt for as long as six months. During that time, what you say will hold more weight than who you are. But everyone will be watching to see if what you say and what you do line up. If you have demonstrated character and competence, your credibility will keep gaining more weight until who you are eventually has greater influence than what you say. As people's trust grows, so will your influence.

To demonstrate competence as you start in leadership, begin with the basics:

- **Work hard:** There is no substitute for a good work ethic. People respect someone who works hard.
- **Think ahead:** Because your decisions affect your team, beginning with the end in mind and identifying priorities are doubly important.
- **Demonstrate excellence:** The better you are at your job, the higher your initial credibility.
- **Follow through:** Good leaders bring things to completion.

To communicate character to team members in a short time, do the following:

- **Care about the people you lead:** Any time new leaders arrive on the scene, the people on the team ask three things: Do they care for me? Can they help me? Can I trust them? If you care about people and show it, they will be able to see your good character.

- **Make things right:** Because new leaders want to impress their people, they sometimes try to hide their mistakes. That is the opposite of what they should do. When decisions don't turn out the way they were intended to, leaders owe their followers an explanation and an apology. That may feel painful in the moment, but it will develop character credibility. If they can also make amends for the mistake, that will be even better.

- **Tell the truth:** When there is consistency between the words and actions of leaders, followers know that leaders can be trusted. Honesty adds integrity to the vision and credibility to the vision caster. In the long run, people appreciate truth—even hard truth.

If you put in the slow hard work of developing credibility through character and competence, you will begin to earn trust. The more trust you gain, the more potential influence you'll have. When the team wins, you gain further credibility. When you make a mistake or the team fails, it costs. Your goal is to earn so much credibility that people buy into your leadership and never lose faith in you, because if they do you've lost credibility with the organization.

How Do You Determine Your Leadership Potential?

I believe that nearly everyone has the potential to lead. Maybe not everyone can become a great leader, but everyone can become a better leader. You need to examine four areas to get a sense of whether it is time for you to step up and lead:

1. Pay Attention to the Need You See

Leadership begins with a need, not when someone wants to fill an empty leadership position. Sometimes people see a need and it sparks something within them, a passion. There are many needs in this world. Are there some that strike a chord in you? If you see a need that you feel a strong desire to address, and it moves you to action, that is a sign that you have the potential to lead in that area.

2. Use Your Natural Abilities to Help Others

When the desire to address a need intersects with an ability to do something about it, sparks begin to fly. When the ability of the leader perfectly fits the need of the moment, the results can be extraordinary. You have gifts, talents, and skills that you can use to help people. It is your responsibility to learn what those abilities are and develop them. If you're not sure what they are, ask others who know you well. In addition, look at the areas where you are naturally intuitive, productive, satisfied, and influential. We tend to lead naturally in areas where we are gifted. We also add the most value when we work in those areas. Once you've discovered and developed your abilities, put them to use to help your team.

3. Make the Most of Your Passion

When you begin helping others in an area that you believe is important, you may find the passion rising in you. That's a positive sign. Passion in a leader is compelling to others. People want to follow passionate leaders. It makes them want to jump on board and join them. If you are new to leadership, tap into your passion and fuel it. If you're not new to leadership, make sure you don't lose your passion. A cold leader never inspired anyone to a cause. A red-hot leader inspires nearly everyone.

4. Develop Your Influence

The bottom line on leadership is that it's influence. If you want to lead, you must persuade people to work with you. People who think they're leading but have no one following them are only taking a walk. If you focus your attention on a need that speaks to your heart, make the most of your abilities, tap into your passion, and develop influence, you can become a leader. And you will be able to make a difference in the world.

How Can I Discover My Unique Purpose as a Leader?

I think all people desire to find the thing for which they would die, because that points them to their purpose. And I think everyone has the potential to discover it. That's especially important for leaders, because their purpose affects the lives of not only themselves, but also of other people.

But discovering your purpose takes time. First you need to know yourself. Your unique purpose must be built on your strengths. Discover your strengths and you have the opportunity to discover your purpose. Don't learn what they are, and you have very little chance of living out your purpose. You can learn a lot from self-evaluation tools, such as StrengthsFinder, but some things you will learn only through trial and error. Every success and every failure can bring you another step closer to knowledge of yourself.

Once you discover your strengths, you must intentionally increase your time using them. That's when you will likely begin seeing themes emerge in your life. Your goals are to sharpen your skills and to increasingly target your work toward your strengths until you home in on the thing that makes you say, "I was born to do this."

What Really Matters to You?

If you're having a difficult time finding your purpose or setting direction for your leadership, ask yourself,

What makes me sing? Your answer reveals what brings you joy.

What makes me cry? Your answer reveals what touches your heart.

What makes me dream? Your answer reveals what sparks your imagination.

What makes me excel? Your answer reveals your strengths.

What makes me different? Your answer reveals your uniqueness.

The more of these questions you can answer, the greater the number of clues you'll have to help you reveal your purpose as a leader.

It takes time to learn about yourself, but it also takes effort to remain true to yourself. People will ask you to depart from the path that's right for you. But the better you know yourself and the truer you are to yourself, the greater your success will be as a leader.

It Is Said That to Be a Good Leader You Must First Be a Good Follower. Does This Maxim Hold True at All Times? If So, at What Point Does a Follower Become a Leader?

This question reveals a common misconception about leading and following. It assumes that it's either-or. It's not. It's both all the time. Nobody does only one or the other. It's an interplay that leaders must navigate from moment to moment.

In many situations I take the lead. I cast vision and set direction for my organizations. But often I become the follower when deferring to the expertise of people in my organization.

Watch the interplay of people during a meeting. In a healthy environment, different people take the lead based on the situation and the skills needed in the moment. Only egotistical leaders believe they must lead in any and every situation. The best leaders know what it's like to follow and have learned how to do it. And they are willing to learn how to follow well before trying to lead.

Good followers add value to an organization. They focus well and do their best to make their team and organization better. They strive for excellence in their work. They spot problems and volunteer to fix them. And they champion new ideas. Successful followership is a learned skill, just as leadership is. If you want to be a good leader, understand following, and never forget what it's like to sit in the follower's chair.

I'm a Bit Introverted. How Can I Accept My Personality, Yet Blossom in Connecting with Others?

Because so much of leadership is about working with people, it can be more difficult for some introverts to get started leading. But that doesn't mean that introverts can't lead. They have led well in every industry and area of life. You don't need to be an extrovert to lead others. However, you may at times have to be more outgoing than you would naturally like to be.

You should not try to change your personality to become a better leader. That will only make you come across as phony. You just need to become your best self by focusing on your gifts and maximizing the best qualities of your temperament. For example, let's look at the two classic introverted temperaments: phlegmatic and melancholic. Phlegmatics are known for their steadiness and their ability as peacemakers. If you're phlegmatic, tap into those qualities to give your team security and stability, and then get people to work together. Melancholics are known for their thinking ability, their creativity, and their attention to detail. If you're melancholic, make the most of those qualities by planning and strategizing.

In addition to using your strengths, you do need to make a deliberate and continuous effort to connect with people. To do that...

1. Understand the Value of Connecting with Others

Few things are more important to the leader-follower relationship than connection. If you want to connect with people, never forget how important it is, and work at it every day. People don't care how much you know until they know how much you care. It may sound corny but it is true.

2. Connect with Others Using Your Strengths

Use your personal strengths to build rapport and relationships with people. I rely on five qualities every day when working with people, whether one-on-one, in a meeting, or onstage:

- **Humor:** I enjoy a good laugh and I don't mind being the butt of the joke.
- **Authenticity:** I am myself in all situations, and I don't teach anything I don't live or believe.
- **Confidence:** I feel good about myself and I believe strongly in people.
- **Hope:** I naturally lift up and encourage people, and I love to do it.
- **Simplicity:** I'm pragmatic, not intellectual. I don't try to impress people with big words or complex sentences. I want to connect with people, so I keep it simple.

I don't know what your strengths are, but you have some. What are your top five? Are you using them? Have you found a way to make who you are work for you?

Leading Different Personalities

Each personality type has its own strengths. Which one are you?

The most natural leaders: Choleric

The most loyal leaders: Phlegmatic

> The most gifted leaders: Melancholic
>
> The most loved leaders: Sanguine
>
> Make the most of your personality type.

3. Ask Good Leaders to Give You Feedback

If you want to learn how to make the most of your strengths and leverage the best traits of your personality type, seek out feedback from other leaders. People who are not good at leadership and communication may be able to tell when you aren't connecting, but only good connectors can tell you why. And only by being yourself and building on your strengths can you become a better leader.

What Advice Would You Give to an Aspiring Leader Trying to Take the First Steps into Leadership?

My best piece of advice would be to try to take the long view of leadership. When you're young, people don't think you're very good. And they don't give you much credit. But if you work hard, learn how to connect with people, develop credibility, and prove yourself every day, after a while people will begin to believe in you. You will have influence, and you will be able to get things done. And here's what's really ironic. Lead well for long enough, and people will shift from giving you *no* credit, to giving you *proper* credit, to giving you *too much* credit. Today, people think I'm better than I actually am.

So try not to worry too much about what people think about you. Do your best. Work hard. Keep growing. And eventually you'll be able to make a positive impact as a leader.

What's the First Thing a Leader Should Do When Brought in from the Outside?

Whenever you take on the responsibility to lead a new team, it's a challenge, whether you are an experienced leader or a novice. But I believe there are five things you can do to get off on the right foot and set up the team for success:

1. Strengthen Relationships

The quickest way to build relationships is to try to get to know and understand each person on your team. To understand the mind of an individual, look at what that person has already achieved. To understand the heart of a person, look at what he or she aspires to do. If you have a handle on people's history and aspirations, you've gone a long way to getting to know them.

2. Earn People's Trust

You cannot lead a team if you do not have the team members' trust. It's always important for a leader to be trustworthy, but it's crucial when you're starting out in the role. Be honest and do what you say you're going to do, and people will gradually give you more trust.

3. Position Team Members Properly

It is the leader's responsibility to position team members where they add the most value and have the greatest chance for success. Doing that serves them individually as well as helping the team to perform at its best. When you take over a team, if you do nothing other than put each player in his or her strength zone, you will greatly increase the productivity and success of the team. It can make a huge difference in a very short time.

4. Create Clear Expectations

Another fairly quick way to positively affect a team is to give the entire team as well as each individual player clear expectations when it comes to performance and goals. Not knowing what's expected of us is confusing and demotivating. We all want to have the "win" defined for us. It's always been my experience that if I expect great things from my people, they'll go to great lengths to keep from disappointing me. Good people always rise to your level of expectation.

5. Determine People's Capacity

If you encourage people to strive to go further than they ever have, and you give them the freedom to fail, they will take risks, and you will help them to determine what their true capacity is. That's no small thing. Daniel H. Pink says, "One source of frustration in the workplace is the frequent mismatch between what people must do and what people can do. When what they must do exceeds their capabilities, the result is anxiety. When what they must do falls short of their capabilities, the result is boredom. But when the match is just right, the results can be glorious."

How Do You Find Balance Between Leading Others and Producing?

Leadership can come as the result of a person's being productive. That's often why people are willing to follow you. If you're good at what you do, motivated people want to know why. They want to watch you and learn from you. They're willing to take your direction, because they hope you can make them better. That's where leadership often starts.

Let's say you're a highly productive person and others begin to recognize that you're good at what you do, and they start asking for your help, even though you have no official leadership responsibilities yet. What do you do? Helping others will take your time. It may reduce your productivity. Will you help them, even though it becomes more difficult for you to take care of your own responsibilities and get your work done? Many people don't want to be bothered. But let's say you love what you do and you desire to help people, so you give them some of your time and pick up the slack by working either longer or smarter. During this season you're probably going to be spending 90 percent of your time producing and only 10 percent leading.

If you work in an organization that recognizes and rewards producers who help the team, you will probably be given some leadership responsibilities. However, you may receive those on top of your other responsibilities. (And this will almost certainly be true if you are an entrepreneur or self-employed.) This is where you need to begin learning how to manage producing and leading. Maybe the balance shifts from 90:10 to 80:20. At this point two things become critical: priorities and delegation. At some point you will run out of hours in your day and days in your week. You will have to stop doing some things and start delegating others. To start figuring out what tasks you can shift, ask yourself these questions:

- **What am I *required* to do personally?** Some tasks cannot be delegated. Ask what *must* be done that *only* you can do and that cannot be delegated. These responsibilities must remain high on your priority list.

- **What gives the organization the greatest *return*?** Some of the things you do return great value to the organization because they use your greatest strengths. These are the things in your production zone, and you should never delegate them to someone else.

- **What *rewards* me personally?** There are certain tasks that we simply enjoy doing. If they bring a high return, great. If not, we need to let them go. If you want to be productive, you should try to learn to get joy from what gives the greatest return and discipline yourself to do those things.

- **What *reproduces* productivity and leadership in others?** When most people think of delegation, they focus on the benefit to themselves. They understand that it frees up their time to take on additional responsibilities, like leading. And that's good. But there is another benefit of delegating: it allows others to grow in their ability to produce or lead. In the beginning, this can actually take up more of your time. But in the long run, it pays off not only for you but also for the organization and the people you develop.

As your leadership ability and responsibilities increase, the balance between the time you spend leading and the time you spend producing will evolve. If you are a great equipper and developer of people, you may get to where you are spending 90 percent of your time leading and reproducing leaders and only 10 percent of your time actually producing. However, if at any point you begin to lose credibility with your team or the person you work for, you will need to shift more time and attention back to producing. Productivity is the engine that drives your credibility and leadership.

I'm Always Worried About Hurting People's Feelings or What They Will Think of Me. What Can I Do to Overcome This and Become a Strong Leader?

As long as you're overly concerned about what other people think of you, you won't be able to become a strong leader. I say that because I used to be a people pleaser and I cared too much about what others thought of me. The key to my change was deciding to do what was best, not what was best for me. I had to believe in the cause more than in my comfort. I had to live for a purpose bigger than myself. I had to be willing to take the heat so that I could move people forward. Here's how this works:

- Believing in the cause creates your conviction.
- Believing in your vision fuels your inspiration.
- Believing in your people builds your motivation.

Once you possess enough conviction to keep you from worrying about what others think, you will be willing and able to set the standards necessary for you to lead effectively. You must listen to others and consider their thoughts and ideas, but do what's right for the organization and the people according to your personal values and the highest standards.

How Does an Emerging Leader Establish Leadership Confidence Without Affirmation?

Confidence makes it possible for leaders to take risks and speak up. It empowers them to go first when they need to. It helps them tackle big problems and overcome failure. Let's face it: leadership is often messy and difficult. Confidence makes it possible for leaders to keep moving forward in spite of this.

Confidence also sets individuals apart. Confident people stand out from the crowd. Confident leaders provide certainty to uncertain people and security to insecure people. People migrate to confident leaders. People want to follow others who know where they're going. Their confidence gives the people who follow them confidence. Together they are more likely to overcome adversity.

Unfortunately, many young leaders have to function in environments where they receive limited guidance and even less affirmation. Because of that, many leaders must learn to develop confidence on their own. That can be difficult, but it's not impossible. If you desire to improve your leadership confidence, do the following:

1. Spend Time with People Who Give You Confidence

Many times we lack confidence because the people we spend the most time with would rather take us down a notch than lift us up. If people in your life make you feel discouraged and tentative, you need to spend less time with them and more time with people who want to see you win and express that to you.

2. Find a Way to Get a Few Wins Under Your Belt

If your confidence isn't what it needs to be, find ways to rack up a few wins. Start with easy ones if you need to. For that matter, you can also make a list of past victories to help you develop (or regain) confidence. Even the best of leaders sometimes feel low and need to remember past victories to give them a boost so they can move forward.

3. Quit Comparing Yourself to Others

One of the things most detrimental to people's confidence is comparing themselves to others. If you are not a naturally confident person or you have a glass-is-half-empty type of personality, you will most likely compare your worst to others' best and find yourself lacking. Don't do it! Others are often not as good as we give them credit for, and we are all too aware of our own weaknesses. As a result, the comparison is distorted. Besides, each of us is a unique individual with something to contribute to this world. Instead of comparing yourself to others, focus on being your best you.

4. Specialize Until You're Special

If you want to gain confidence, become an expert in something. If you specialize in doing something based on one of your top strengths, you not only add value to your team, you also find it easier to believe in yourself. Develop a valuable skill. Become an expert on your product. Learn everything there is to know about your customers. It can be nearly anything—if it helps the team to succeed and it gives you confidence, it's a win for everybody.

There is no one clear path to leadership. There is no simple checklist for becoming a leader. Each person's journey is different. I learned many great lessons in my first leadership position, the most important of which was that leadership has to be earned. Leaders have to grow into their roles, and if the role becomes more demanding, the leader has to keep growing. Leadership is never a right. It's a privilege and a responsibility. But it's one that is open to anyone who's willing to work hard enough to get it.

4

How to Resolve Conflicts and Lead Challenging People

Dealing with conflict and leading challenging people is one of the most difficult areas for most leaders. You can do all the right things, but there is no guarantee others will change, succeed, or do well. The recommendations in this chapter will work only with people who possess some desire to work with you. People who do not want to follow or be productive members of the team will not change. And that doesn't make you a bad leader. It just means you have someone who's bad for the team and organization. You cross into bad leadership only if you make the choice to keep someone on the team when you shouldn't.

Too often, leaders wait. They don't like to make these difficult decisions. They hope people will change on their own instead of challenging them and offering them a pathway to change. This rarely works. Everyone deserves our best shot as leaders to help them succeed. But they don't deserve repeated chances—especially at the expense of others on the team. Nobody likes making these hard decisions, but they must be made, and the sooner the better. Good leaders are direct and decisive in these matters. Ask yourself: is this best for the team? If keeping someone who's difficult isn't, get him or her off the team.

How Can a Leader Deal with a Difficult Member of the Team?

How do you move an individual from unteachable to teachable? Demand the change of a bad attitude from an employee? Lead someone with a passive-aggressive personality who is loyal and effective but is hindering the team? Handle an angry employee? Or deal with a person who does not want to be led?

Any time you have difficulty with people you lead, whether it's because of a negative attitude, poor performance, lack of cooperation, or some other issue, you need to start a process, and that process is the same for nearly every situation. Before I lay that out for you, I want to point out two questions you need to ask before you get started:

Can they change? This deals with ability.
Will they change? This deals with attitude.

Most of the questions in this chapter about dealing with others do not relate to ability. They relate to attitude.

For this process to be successful, when you ask people to change, the answer to both questions has to be yes. It can't be either-or. I've known people with great ability but a bad attitude, and I've known people with a great attitude and poor ability. If people are able and willing to change, there's a chance you can be successful.

1. Meet Privately ASAP to Discuss Their Behavior

Most people wait too long to address an issue with an employee. That's a mistake. If you have a problem with someone, do something about it as quickly as you can.

Meet with the person privately and level with them with integrity and honesty. Clearly lay out what the issue is, giving specific, tangible examples of the undesirable actions or behaviors. Don't be vague. Don't use secondhand reports. Don't attribute bad motives to them, because they will only get defensive. Never go into one of these meetings angry. If you do, you greatly reduce your chances of success. In fact, go into the conversation assuming their motives are good. This is more likely to make them open to change and willing to make corrections. And be sure to explain how their actions are negatively affecting the organization, the team, or you.

If your attitude is positive, your mind-set is to give them the benefit of the doubt, and you truly want to help the person, you give yourself the best odds for a positive resolution.

2. Ask for Their Side of the Story

Sometimes circumstances such as a personal tragedy are temporarily prompting unwanted behavior, and the person simply needs help or understanding. That's why you don't want to go in with guns blazing. You might be wrong.

3. Try to Come to a Place of Agreement

At this point it's time to find out if they agree with you. Admitting they're in the wrong can be very humbling for them, but it opens them up to change, and that's ideal. Often you can help someone with that attitude.

However, I've had many people say, "No, it's someone else's problem." When that happens, I tell them, "I believe I'm right and this is your problem. I'm going to give you a week to think about it. We'll meet again and discuss it." My hope is that they'll give it some honest thought and maybe ask people who know them well and will be honest with them.

After a week has gone by, we meet and I ask, "Do you agree that this is your problem?" If they have had a change of heart and agree with me, we can move forward to the next step, because they've taken responsibility. If they still don't agree, I say, "You may not agree with what I've just said. But you will have to agree to change and follow my guidelines if you want to remain on the team. And I'm going to hold you accountable."

4. Set Out a Future Course of Action with a Deadline

No matter whether people agree with you or not, you must lay out a specific course of action for them to take. Once again, be very specific. Indicate any actions they must not take or behaviors they must not exhibit, starting immediately. If there are action steps they will need to follow through on, lay those out and put deadlines on them. And make sure they understand. Put your requirements into writing if needed. If you don't both agree on what needs to happen in the future, you will both be frustrated.

5. Validate the Value of the Person and Express Your Commitment to Help

Before you finish your meeting, let them know that you care about them and genuinely desire a positive resolution to the situation. Tell them how you will help them. Sometimes the greatest value a leader can add to other people comes through telling them the truth, showing them where they can grow, and then helping them change. Some people spend years on a job being resented by their boss and fellow employees, but are never told about their problem or given a chance to change and grow. As a leader, you have the chance to help them.

Sitting down with people and telling them where they fall short isn't easy. And there's no guarantee that they will acknowledge their problem or change. There's a strong chance that you will have to let them go. If you are having a hard time making that decision, ask yourself this question: "If I needed to hire new people, knowing what I know now, would I hire these individuals?"

If the answer is yes—keep them.

If the answer is no—let them go.

If the answer is maybe—reevaluate in three months.

If the answer is that you don't know, give yourself three months. If after that the answer is still that you don't know, the answer is really no. Your emotions are making it difficult for you to accept a hard decision. As a leader, you owe it to the rest of the team to make these tough choices. That's what you get paid for.

How Do You Raise the Bar When People Have Gotten Used to Settling for Mediocrity?

The first question in this chapter dealt primarily with attitude issues. This is more of a performance issue. I think any time the team isn't performing, the leader has to look at himself first. You need to examine whether you might be part of the problem. Are you setting a bad example? Have you lowered your expectations so far that people just assume that average is OK? If either of these things is true, go back to the question in chapter one: why does leading myself seem more difficult than leading others? You can't raise the bar for others if you haven't raised the bar for yourself.

If you as a leader are pushing to reach your maximum potential, you can begin to look at the people you lead and start asking them questions:

- **Are you reaching your maximum potential?** Many people don't understand that they can do much more than they are currently doing. Help them see the possibilities.

- **Would you like to do better?** If they answer yes, you may be able to help them. If they answer no, they can't even help themselves.

- **Do you know how to reach your maximum potential?** This is a case where a "no" answer is actually a good thing. If they don't know the path forward, you may be able to show it to them.

- **Can I help you?** One of the most rewarding roles leaders have is that of coach and mentor. When people are teachable and open to growth, helping them succeed can be highly rewarding.

As a leader you need to help your people understand that nothing good comes out of being average professionally. You can't build a business or make a difference by being average. One of the best ways to raise the bar for people is to do it incrementally. For example, if you are a real estate broker with a lot of agents in your office and most of them make only three sales a year, challenge them to do four. That's a very reasonable increase that most people will believe they can do. If you set the goal, give them an incentive to reach it, help them create a plan to achieve it, and check in with them along the way, most of them will be able to achieve it.

The beauty of incremental challenges is that they increase the confidence of the people who achieve them. And they inspire everyone else who has been average. They give them hope. That's why every time someone gets a win, you should tell their story. It rewards that person and motivates those in the middle to perform better. The top producers don't need motivation. They are already motivated and performing well. Everyone else needs it.

An incremental challenge also helps the organization when it has a lot of people. If every person grows a little, the organization grows a lot. If you can get a lot of people improving, it can have a tremendous impact overall.

How Do You Motivate an Unmotivated Person?

When I started out in leadership, I thought I could change people. Now I realize I can't. People must change themselves. That doesn't mean that I have no responsibility to people in my organization in the area of motivation. There are still things I can do. I can work to create an environment and culture where motivation is valued and rewarded. Here are the ways I do that:

Start with Motivated People

The best way to create a culture of motivation is to start with as many motivated people as you can. And if you want people on your team to be motivated, you must be motivated yourself. People do what people see.

You should also hire motivated people. That sounds obvious, but you might be surprised how many leaders leave this trait out of the equation when looking for team members. Many focus too much on just talent or skill. Even the leaders who recognize the importance of attitude sometimes miss motivation.

Understand the Connection Between Relationships and Motivation

People are motivated by leaders who connect with them and treat them like human beings. If you are a people person, this may sound painfully obvious to you, yet some leaders still miss it. I once knew a leader who referred to all the people on his team as "ding-a-lings." It was clear that he believed everyone was below him. His contempt for people was apparent to everyone who worked for him. Few things are more demotivating than working for someone who disrespects you.

Hire Motivated People

How can you identify motivated people? They usually have several of the following traits:

1. They exhibit a positive attitude.

2. They can articulate specific goals for their life.

3. They are initiators.

4. They have a proven track record of success.

Look for these traits when looking for new team members.

Give Each Person a Reputation to Uphold

People often go further than they think they can go when someone else thinks they can. One way to show people that you believe in them and in the possibility of success for their future is to give them a reputation to uphold.

Ask yourself what's special, unique, and wonderful about each person on your team. All people have talents, skills, and positive traits that make them valuable to the team. Figure out what they are and then share them with others. The more you validate people for the good things they do—or could do—the more they want to do them. Not only does this motivate them to perform in their strength, it also encourages an environment where people say positive things about one another.

Reward What You Want Done

Rewards are motivating. Rules, consequences, and punishment don't do anything to get people going. They merely keep people from doing their worst. If you want people's best, give them incentives for performance.

How Do You Deal with People Who Start Things but Never Finish?

The bookends of success are starting and finishing. Some people never start. If people don't have the discipline to do what they must when they need to do it, they have no shot at success. Good things in life don't float to you. However, some people are in love with starting things, but never finish them. As a leader you can help people to finish better by helping them understand what happens when they don't follow through and finish something:

They Lose the Reward of Finishing

Anyone who has accomplished things in life understands that 90 percent of the rewards in life come on the back end, not the front end. A great sense of personal satisfaction comes from completing a job and doing it well. There is a real feeling of camaraderie and joy among team members when they work together to accomplish a goal. And of course the monetary rewards also come from finishing. People who never finish anything never experience these rewards, so they don't understand them.

They Lower Their Self-Esteem

Every time people quit and don't finish something they start, they lose a bit of their self-esteem. Whether they are aware of it or not, they begin to internally label themselves as quitters. I've never found a person with a high self-image who quits all the time. There is a pride in accomplishment that people who quit do not possess. They may show false bravado, but not a deep sense of satisfaction with who they are and what they can do.

They Sabotage Their Own Success

People who never finish often don't understand they are developing a habit that will sabotage their success. Quitting becomes a habit. And they make excuses. But it's easier to move from failure to success than from excuses to success!

They Lose the Trust and Respect of Others

Quit enough times, and others will think you are unreliable, and that erodes trust. Nobody wants to work with people they cannot trust. Nobody wants to be handcuffed to a quitter. People who blow themselves up will eventually take you with them.

Practical Tips to Help People Become Finishers

To help people learn to finish what they start, do the following:

1. **Show them the big picture:** Help them to see the more positive future they can have if they learn to become finishers.

2. **Give them accountability:** People who have developed the habit of quitting are often unaccountable for their actions. You can change that.

3. **Help them schedule their time:** People who don't finish are often unorganized or undisciplined. They often need tools to help them with scheduling tasks.

4. **Provide a work partner:** Sometimes pairing non-finishers with highly motivated people can help them to follow through. Just be sure you don't bring down a good performer in the process.

5. **Reward only finished work:** It's good to praise effort, but you should never reward it. Give the reward only when the work is done.

People who don't finish what they start often don't recognize the negative impact it has on themselves and others. As a leader, you can help them to understand. Teach them that by starting *and* finishing they are demonstrating that they can handle bigger and better responsibilities. They become candidates for more time, attention, and opportunity from you and the organization because they are demonstrating that they are ready for these things.

How Can Leaders Help Individuals Move Past Mistakes and Get on a Path of Success Toward a Better Future?

The ability to deal with difficulties, mistakes, failure, and loss is crucial to people's success. Many people get emotionally stuck when they make a mistake or suffer a loss. They often become overwhelmed by regret. If the regret takes hold for too long, it can turn into guilt, resentment, and self-pity. When we experience losses, we need to learn from them and let them go. If we focus on the loss instead, it can bring us down.

Some losses require time because they cut deeply. We need to grieve. We need time to heal. But many small losses and problems don't warrant much energy.

One of the healthiest ways to treat loss is the same way we should treat victory: observe the twenty-four-hour rule. When we experience victory, we should celebrate for no longer than twenty-four hours. When we experience defeat, we should let it get us down for no longer than twenty-four hours. Once you've processed the emotions, it's time to learn from the experience and move on.

At What Point Do You Turn Your Energy Away from Low Performers and Focus on Those Who Want to Grow?

As leaders, we often want to take everyone with us. But some people can't go with you. Others don't want to. Your job as a leader is to give people a chance to get on board, giving them your best at helping them succeed, or to move on without them.

The people you spend most of your time and energy on are the ones who stay. The ones you neglect are the ones who leave. If you give your effort to the negative people, at some point you need to ask yourself how much of your energy, time, focus, joy, and resources you'll let them take. There is a cost to keeping negative or unproductive people. There are lifters and leaners. Whom do you want on your team? If you don't winnow out the dissenters and low performers, you lose people's respect for your leadership. If people are not doing their jobs, they deserve your best shot to help them succeed. If they're still not doing their best when you have given them your best shot, it's time to make changes.

As a leader, you have to set the standard and then follow through on it. You have to be willing to make the difficult choices and live with the fallout.

When I have to let someone go, I try to do it in the right way. I appreciate them. I do the right thing financially. And I don't look back. Recently, when I let someone go, he wanted another chance or the opportunity to come back in a lesser role. I said no. If it doesn't work, it doesn't work. Often we know it won't work, but we want to keep the relationship and we give in. That's not good for anybody in the long run.

How Do You Inspire Your Team to Make Its Current Work a Career and Not Just Another Job with a Paycheck?

If you're leading people who have settled into a role or position, whether it's because they are in a comfort zone or because they see their work as just a job, try to help them open their eyes and think beyond today. Help them to realize that a job is never big enough for a human being. We have too much inside us for that. Offer them something beyond their job by doing the following:

Share Your Passion

If you have passion for what you do, you need to share it with your people. A leader's passion is contagious. It can attract other passionate people, and it can spark a flame in people who might not otherwise be passionate. If they can understand and connect with the vision you have and the passion you feel, there's a good chance that they will catch it and become passionate too.

Paint a Picture of a Better Future

People want to make a difference. One of your jobs as a leader is to paint a picture of their future that inspires them to work harder today. Tell them who they can become. Show them what they could someday be doing. This must be done with integrity, because as leaders, we never want to manipulate people. We just want to help them envision the future.

Show How Their Role Makes a Difference

Too often people don't understand how their tasks contribute to the bigger picture. Good leaders help team members understand their role. They help them see how their contribution is making a difference. This gives team members a sense of ownership over the mission, and inspires them to do better work.

Challenge Them to Keep Growing

We need to help people see the value of growing. It is essential not only for the organization's viability, but also for the individual's future. People who make growth their goal—instead of a title, position, salary, or other external target—always have a future.

All of these things have the potential to help a leader inspire someone to invest himself more fully in his or her work and stop coasting. But everything I've just discussed rests on one assumption: that you are passionate about your own work. That is essential. People do not follow an uncertain trumpet. They can't catch fire from a leader who has grown cold himself. If you aren't fired up, you are a big part of the problem, and the first person you must address is yourself.

How Does One Lead People Who Are More Knowledgeable, or Superior Leaders, When Put in Charge of Them?

If you've been put in charge of a group of people who are stronger than you in leadership or technical ability, here's the good news: you have a position. Here's the bad news: the position won't mean anything to them. They won't follow you because of it.

If the team is talented, you can't fool them. You can't fake it. Good leaders will sniff this out instantly. You can't make a mess and then expect the team to bail you out. You'll lose them. You also can't use your position or pull rank and keep their respect. If you try to, they will disdain you and then sabotage you. You need to admit where they're better than you, and look for common ground. If they know that *you* know you're not as good as they are, they may not feel as compelled to keep pointing it out to you.

Your best strategy may be to enlist help from the most influential person on the team. Go to him or her and say, "Look, I know you're more experienced than I am. You have more knowledge. My goal is to help the team win. Can I get your help? When I have a problem, can I come to you for advice? When I need to make a decision for the team, can I talk it over with you? I know that with your help, we can all be successful." If the person says yes, follow through. Ask for advice. Ask for help. And when things go right, publicly give that person credit.

Who Is Most Influential?

It can be very difficult to evaluate leaders who are more gifted and skilled than you are. It's always easier to judge those less talented. So how do you figure out who the main influencer is? Ask these questions:

1. When points are being made, whom does everyone agree with?

2. When questions are asked, whom does everyone look to for answers?

3. When conflict arises, whom does everyone defer to?

4. Who is the person everybody listens to when he or she speaks?

You may not be able to make this determination quickly. You may need to see people interacting in a variety of situations over time. But if you pay attention, you should be able to figure it out.

How Long Do You Push Someone's Potential When They Are Not Reaching It?

To keep growing toward our potential, we have to be intentional. We have to fight for it. That can be difficult. Not everyone is willing to keep doing it. When people stop growing, I find that it is often for one or more of the following reasons:

Choices

Many people make choices that limit them. They quit a job with great potential because it is difficult. They put themselves into debt and then can't pursue an entrepreneurial opportunity. They choose a fun vacation over a conference that might lead to a personal breakthrough. In life, for everything you gain, you give up something. We can make choices that increase our potential or choices that take away from it.

Time

Most people have a short-term approach to success. They want it now. And even if they are willing to engage in a process, they usually have no idea it will take a long time. So they bail out. I have to admit, I am an impatient person and usually have unrealistic expectations about how long something will take. So I develop systems to help me, and I rely on daily disciplines. By focusing on what I know I should do today, I am able to keep plugging away and continue growing.

Price

Many people think they can rely on talent alone to get them through life. But talent will not carry you to your potential.

It's only one part of the equation. Everyone who strives to reach his or her potential must pay a price—in time, effort, resources, and opportunities missed. Many people fail to pay the price that their potential demands.

Problems

Everybody faces problems, obstacles, and barriers. Some people let those things defeat them. They fail to think creatively when problems arise. They don't have the tenacity to fight through them. Or they lack belief in themselves. Sometimes all people need is some encouragement. Spend time getting to know what a person can do.

Most people do not push themselves to their full capacity to reach their potential. If you lead people who are falling short of their potential, you need to start asking why. Have you put them in their strength zone? Are you providing the training and resources they need to be successful? Is there something they need that you're not giving? You always need to make sure you are not the problem before you look to see where the problem is.

After that, you must remember it is their choice, not yours. You can't push people to reach their potential. You can choose to leave the door open for them, but they must walk through. If they choose not to, you're better off spending your time on someone who's hungry and actively wants to grow.

How Do You Know a Relationship Is Broken, and How Can You Save It?

Any time a relationship is strained, damaged, or broken, address the problem as quickly as possible. When something is broken or a person is hurt, when there's silence between you, the other person almost always assumes the worst. And they start filling any gaps of information with negative assumptions.

How can you tell when a relationship has become broken? These are the most common signs:

- **It's hard to have an honest conversation:** They don't want to hear from you. They don't want to talk it out. Maybe they've been so hurt that they just can't handle it.

- **There's a lack of trust:** The other person begins to question motives. Maybe they feel a sense of injustice or lack of fairness. Whatever trust was originally there begins to deteriorate.

- **There's a lack of passion to continue the relationship:** The other person stops putting in any effort to build back the relationship or make it work. They may withdraw completely. Even if you're together, you're not relating to each other.

When you see these signs, you should try to repair the relationship. That doesn't mean trying to get it back at all

costs. Some people sell themselves to try to buy back a broken relationship, and they give away too much. Your goal should be to repair the relationship but to do it with integrity. Here's what I think it takes to do that:

1. Initiate Fixing the Relationship with Them

I think it's always the leader's responsibility to be the first to try to mend the relationship. We need to pick up the phone and say, "Hey, can we go to lunch? We need to talk." That doesn't mean it always pays off. But it's hard to rescue a relationship if you don't take responsibility for initiating.

2. Give Them the Benefit of the Doubt

I always go into that conversation assuming that I've done something wrong. I've discovered that if there's hope for helping a relationship come back, the conversation goes better if I'm open and willing to take the blame. So I assume I'm wrong. I'll ask, "Have I offended you? Is there something I've done that's put a strain on our relationship? Is there anything I can do to make amends? Please talk to me."

Sometimes people say, "No, it's not you," and they'll explain what's going on in their life that is causing them to withdraw. Sometimes they say, "Yes, there is. Here's what you did." And they'll talk to me. When that happens, there's a chance to repair the relationship. When that's the case, I ask forgiveness. And even if what I did wasn't wrong, I still apologize for what hurt them. It's difficult to move forward with relational baggage weighing you down.

3. Be Willing to Walk the Second Mile

I believe it is the responsibility of the leader to initiate and to go the second mile in trying to repair a broken relationship. Leaders need to be quick to say, "I'm sorry." They need to be willing to make needed changes. That's a part of leadership.

In relationships, I believe the stronger person is the first one to come back and offer to reconcile. The stronger person is the first to ask for forgiveness. Usually that's the leader. Even if the leader has been the injured party, he or she needs to initiate. However, the truth is that the weaker person controls the relationship. They always do and they always will.

There will be times when no matter how much effort you put in, the relationship is never the same as it was before. And you can't be held hostage by that. You have to accept it because, as a leader, you have the responsibility to be a good steward of your team or organization. You cannot allow your personal feelings of not wanting to hurt somebody keep you from doing what's best for the organization. That was hard for me to learn, because I'm so relationally driven.

4. Speak Well of Them Afterward

After I've talked to people and tried to resolve whatever issues we've had, my goal is to have no unfinished business with them. Whether we resolved the issues and mended the relationship or had to part ways, I don't want there to be any kind of grudge between us, and I want to say only positive things about them.

I think a lot of relationships are worth saving, but many can't be saved. We have to learn to say to ourselves, *It's OK. I don't have to keep this close relationship with this person anymore.* You have to be secure in your leadership and give yourself permission to have a different relationship from what you had before. You still value the person, but you let them go.

5

How to Succeed Working Under Poor Leadership

Many people struggle working for those who aren't any good as leaders, or working with leaders less talented than they are. It's a source of endless frustration. Everything rises and falls on leadership. If you work for a bad leader, you probably feel like it mostly falls...on you!

My assumption going into this chapter is that you've already tried to be cooperative and work things out with the leader. The process I share is designed to force the issue. And I'll be very candid with you. Sometimes it works. Sometimes it doesn't. You have no control over that. You can only control what you do and how you respond. If everything goes well, you've made a tremendous breakthrough. If things don't go the way you hoped or planned, it may be time to move on. If you decide to stay and try to make the best of the situation, I provide a few strategies for the most common problems related to difficult leaders.

I believe leaders are responsible for whom and what they lead. Bad bosses often shirk their responsibilities and try to place them on the follower—on you—and you end up carrying the load. Whenever this happens, you should, as far as it's possible, attempt to ask questions of your leader in such a way that the responsibility goes back on his or her shoulders, where it belongs.

How Can You Succeed with a Leader Who Is Difficult to Work With?

If you are working for a bad or difficult leader, and you intend to try to improve the situation, you need to do your homework and go through a deliberate process to seek resolution. Though each problem is unique, the process for trying to reach a positive solution is similar in nearly all circumstances. It will increase your chances for a positive outcome. However, you need to go into the process with realistic expectations. Many poor leaders do not respond well to having their methods questioned. So part of what you will be doing is preparing yourself for what you will do if it doesn't go well.

That doesn't mean you should shrink from the task, especially if interaction with your leader is causing a violation of your values, the erosion of your confidence, or the undermining of your ability to achieve success in your work. You need to move forward. Here is how I suggest you proceed:

1. Consider Whether You *Might Actually Be the Problem*

It's often easy to point out all the things that someone else is doing wrong, but when we do that, we sometimes neglect to examine ourselves to see what *we* are doing wrong. If I want to try to solve a problem with someone else, I need first to own up to my part in it and work to fix it. So before you start looking at what's wrong with your leader, first determine what's wrong with you.

2. Determine Whether You Have Specific Evidence to Support Your Opinion

Before you decide to meet with your leader, you need to be sure the conflict or problem you see is based on solid evidence—not merely your feelings, not hearsay from someone else, not conjecture. Exactly what actions has your leader taken that are wrong? What specific words did you hear your leader say that were offensive or derogatory? Be specific and try to examine them rationally, without emotion. If you can't be specific, you may be wrong in your assessment of the situation.

Why It's Important to Be Specific

The higher the stakes, the more important it is that you have solid, specific evidence.

- The more important the message, the more important it is to give evidence.

- The more important the person, the more important it is to give evidence.

- The more important the timing, the more important it is to give evidence.

3. Assess Your Influence and Credibility with Your Leader

You can be right and have all your facts lined up, but if you have no influence with your leader, you may not get anywhere. Even if what you say is correct, if you have little credibility in the eyes of your leader, the perception may be that your observations have no truth. So before you try to do anything to address the issue, you need to figure out where you stand with him or her. What kind of clout do you have? If you're not sure where you stand, talk to your coworkers. Ask them how much weight they think your words carry with the boss. If you have some degree of credibility, your leader might be willing to listen when you have difficult or negative things to say.

4. Think Through Every Possible Outcome

When most people are unhappy with their leader and their situation at work, they go to their coworkers to complain. By planning to talk to your leader instead, you are trying to do the right thing. But you should have the discussion with your leader only if you are willing to accept the outcome. That means you need to take the time to think about all the different responses your leader might give you and determine what you would do in every instance. If you put in the time, think things through, anticipate the possible reactions of your leader, and know what you will do in any given situation, you are as prepared as you can be.

5. Make a Decision to Act

At this point you have a decision to make. To do things the right way, you need to either take action or accept your situation as it is. If you decide not to take action, move on and don't say anything negative to others about your situation. Never complain about what you allow. If you do, that puts *you* in the wrong. If you are in a situation that's bad for you, you need to act.

6. Ask to Speak with Your Leader Privately

One of the worst mistakes you can make with difficult leaders is to criticize them or call them out publicly. That always turns into a lose-lose proposition. Just as you would hope that your leader would take you aside to share criticism, you should do the same with him or her.

7. Meet, Outline Your Complaint, and Seek a Collaborative Solution

When you meet with your leader, your goal should not be to vent or get even. The point is not to complain. The point is to seek a positive resolution. Present your evidence in a way that is as positive, non-threatening, and non-accusatory as possible. Explain why you find it difficult to work and get your job done, and ask if there is anything that you and your leader can do to resolve the situation and work together more positively.

If you are honest, yet treat your leader with respect, at the end of the discussion you can walk away from the meeting with your integrity intact, no matter what the outcome is. Hopefully you and your leader will be able to agree upon a course of action that will serve both of you well. If your leader refuses to accept responsibility, becomes defensive, or proposes something you're not sure you can agree to, ask for time to think it over. You can always meet again later to try again for a positive solution. If he or she suggests something that you know is good and right, that's great. Move forward with it.

8. Determine Whether You Should Stay or It's Time to Move On

You will have to make a decision after you meet with your leader. Will you stay or will you go? Maybe your leader says he will change. If that turns out to be true, great. Maybe he says he will not change. Are you willing to live with that? Maybe the conversation you had with your leader did further damage to the relationship. In the end you may not be able to change the people around you, but you can change the people you choose to be around.

If you're still having a hard time trying to decide whether to stay or go, ask yourself this question: if I weren't already working here, knowing what I know now, would I want to become part of this organization? If the answer is no, it's time to go. If the answer is "I don't know," ask yourself again in six months. If the answer is yes, stay and learn how to work with your leader.

9. If You Decide You Can Stay, Give Your Best and Publicly Support Your Leader

If you think that you might want to stay and keep working with your leader, you need to ask yourself two crucial questions:

Will I be able to add value?
Will I be able to stay true to myself?

If you cannot answer yes to both of those questions, it would be better for you to leave. But if you can add value and stay true to yourself, you need to publicly support your leader. Stay quiet about the negative things you know about him or her. When you're tempted to say something negative, say something nice instead. And if you need to discuss a problem or address a difficulty, do it behind closed doors. You should never do anything that compromises your integrity, but you need to remain supportive after the discussion.

How Would You Work with a Difficult Leader Who Doesn't Like You?

It's difficult to work with someone you think doesn't like you, especially when it's your leader. Most people don't respond to it well. They often do one of the following:

- **Hide from the person:** Many people go into avoidance mode. There isn't direct conflict, but when we spend our energy hiding, we lose momentum.

- **Hinder the person:** We don't do anything directly destructive. We just make sure not to be very cooperative. This hurts the team and causes us to be unfocused.

- **Harm the person:** The worst of all responses is to try to punish or harm the person who doesn't like us. That causes us to lose integrity.

Instead you need to take the high road. You cannot control your leader's response to you. He or she may never love working with you. But you can do everything in your power to make sure that you are not the cause of the problem. You do that by . . .

Processing Your Emotions

Over time, if your negative emotions are left unchecked and allowed to brew, they will overflow into every area of your working—and maybe also your private—life. These negative emotions can influence our decision making, taint how we view relationships, and affect how we lead our people. For that reason we need to feel our emotions regularly. We must acknowledge how we feel, work through any hurt feelings, and move on.

Looking for Common Ground

Everyone sees the world from their own unique perspective. Whenever and wherever possible, look for points of agreement with your leader. And when you find them, focus on those things you have in common rather than the differences that set you apart. If you are united in a common goal, start there.

Being Consistently Pleasant

Have you ever heard the phrase "Kill them with kindness"? People often soften if you stay constant when they are not—when you are sincere, kind, helpful, and pleasant despite their choices and behavior. And remember, as poet Kahlil Gibran asserted, "Tenderness and kindness are not signs of weakness and despair, but manifestations of strength and resolution."

Solving Problems

One of the best ways to endear yourself to a leader is to be a good problem solver. It's easy to see and point out problems. It's much more difficult—and valuable—to offer and implement solutions. Adding value to others always works to your advantage. If you increase your value by becoming good at offering and implementing solutions, it will make your boss's job easier, and his or her attitude toward you might soften.

Going the Extra Mile

If you want to please people, go above and beyond expectations. Most of the differences between average and top people can be explained in three words: "and then some." If you do your job and then some, people will be drawn to you, maybe even your boss.

Sometimes people dislike another person without good reasons. That could be the case with you and your leader. All you can do is try to connect on common ground and be a great employee. It's difficult to dislike someone who consistently treats people with kindness, does the job well, and goes above and beyond what is expected. If you do all those things and your leader still doesn't like you, you can take comfort in knowing that you are probably not the cause of the problem.

How Would You Work with a Difficult Leader Who Lacks Vision?

Much dissatisfaction and discouragement are caused by absence of vision. Without it, leaders lack the ability to convey motivation, drive, and purpose to their people.

If you are going to stay and work under a leader who lacks vision, what can you do?

Tap into the Organization's Larger Vision

If you work for a larger organization in which your boss is only one leader among many, you can tap into the vision of the organization itself. When the vision of the organization is clear, the vision of any individual leader, team, or department within the organization should contribute to that larger vision anyway. It should work within that context.

How does your team or department support that larger vision of the organization? In what way does your team or department add the most value? How can you advance the purpose of the organization in a significant way? How can you make it better?

Identify a Vision for the Organization and Share It with Your Leader

If you work in a smaller organization where your leader is the top leader, you may want to work at discovering and developing a vision for the organization that will help it succeed. Once you've done that, you can share it with your leader, and if your level of influence is strong, your leader might embrace it and buy into it. If you do this, just be sure that the vision is consistent with the values and goals you know your leader possesses. If it's not, your leader will probably not welcome it.

Develop Your Own Sense of Purpose

Purpose gives you drive. It shows you a destination. It paints a picture of your future. It energizes you. And it makes obstacles and problems seem small in comparison to its importance.

You cannot allow your leader's lack of vision to keep you from making progress in life. Connect with and develop your own purpose. As long as you are doing work consistent with it, you won't be as bothered by your leader's lack of vision for the organization. You will just need to be certain that you are doing what you were created to do.

Vision is critical to good leadership. I have yet to meet a great leader who lacks vision. Any organization whose top leadership lacks vision is in trouble. Further down the leadership chain, is it ideal to have leaders without vision? No. But it is possible for someone to lead up in the organization to influence a leader without vision. It isn't easy, but it is possible.

How Would You Work with a Difficult Leader Who Is Indecisive and Inconsistent?

If you can see solutions within arm's reach, yet your leader prevents you from implementing them, you will be continually frustrated. What can you do to deal with this situation?

Ask Permission to Make the Decisions

Leadership decisions should always be made at the lowest possible level. The people on the front lines usually know the problems and solutions best. They are also closest to the problems and can usually act quickly. So if you know what decisions should be made, ask your leaders if they are willing to let you make them. If they seem unsure, offer to start small with minor decisions that won't make or break the team. In that way you can develop credibility and a positive track record. If they say yes and you're willing to take responsibility for your own decisions and actions, the problem is solved.

Offer to Help Your Leaders Process Decisions

If you are good at decision making and can see solutions readily, but your leaders don't want to release you to act independently, offer to process decisions with them privately. Gather information and present it to them. Define each problem as specifically as you can. Offer a variety of solutions, taking into account their values, motivations, priorities, and goals. Explain the implications of every decision as you see them. Then ask for a decision.

If they are unwilling to come to a conclusion, ask for feedback. Try to find which solutions they prefer and which they dismiss out of hand. In this way you can find out how they think and try to narrow down the options. If they still won't make a decision, try to get them to commit to a deadline. Then circle back later to try to land the decision.

Ask What You Are to Do When a Decision Must Be Made

If you have leaders who will not allow you to either make the decisions or help them make them, your only course of action is to be very direct with them and privately ask the question, "What do you want me to do when a decision *must* be made but you aren't making it?" Likewise, if you work with inconsistent leaders, you must ask a similar question when they change their minds: "Previously you decided that; how do you want me to proceed now that you've decided this?"

By asking these questions, you are putting the ball back in your leaders' court, where it belongs. They are the ones responsible for making decisions. But if they don't take responsibility, at least you have a course of action that they have asked you to take in those situations, and when they change their minds again, you can say with integrity, "The last time we talked, you said you wanted me to do this, and that's what I've done."

How Would You Work with a Difficult Leader Who Has Attitude and Character Problems?

One of the great dangers in working for leaders who have attitude and character problems is that they are continually trying to drag you down to wherever they are. Bad attitudes are contagious. It's difficult to remain positive when people around you are continually negative. And people who cheat or cut corners in their lives will inevitably ask you to do the same, and they won't want to take no for an answer when you refuse to share their methods. It will be a constant struggle for you to retain a positive attitude and maintain your values.

If you are determined to stay in such an environment, the best thing you can try to do is lift people to a higher level. Here's how you can do that:

Live on a Higher Level Yourself

You don't want to allow others' compromises to influence you to compromise your own values. But that alone is not enough. One of your goals as a leader and person should always be to be a positive influence on others in the critical areas of attitude and character. If your leaders aren't strong in these areas, try to lead up and help them as well as your peers and those you lead.

Hold yourself to the highest possible standard. You cannot take people where you haven't been. As you gain a reputation for being positive and reliable by maintaining high standards for yourself, your credibility will increase, and so will your influence. You may have opportunities to help others to realize there's a better way to do things and to make better choices.

Separate Yourself from Negative Influences as Much as Possible

Trying to help others to be positive and honest using influence alone doesn't always work. People have been given free will and make their own choices in life. If you've done your best to help your leaders but you start to feel their influence negatively affecting your attitude or values, separate yourself from them as much as you can. If time and distance don't seem to be helping, consider leaving your position. No job is worth trading your integrity for.

Put Things in Writing Whenever Possible

To a great extent you can avoid a bad attitude. However, you need to protect yourself from someone who has no integrity. The best way to do that is to leave so you don't become party to anything unethical. But if you can't leave right away, or if you need to stay for some reason, put as much communication as you can in writing. You will want to be able to show evidence of your right-doing if at some point your boss is accused of wrongdoing.

How Would You Work with a Difficult Leader Who Acts Like a Bully?

Having bosses who act like bullies makes life difficult. Nobody likes to feel pushed around. If you decide to stay in such an environment, your best bet is to try to let what they say roll off you. Don't buy into what they're selling. That's not going to be easy, so here are some suggestions to help you:

1. Be Confident in Your Own Value

Leaders cannot devalue you without your permission. Unpleasant bosses can say anything they want to you or about you, but if it isn't true, you don't need to buy into it. You prevent that by seeing the value in yourself and being confident in it.

You have value. Every person does. You have talents and skills that can add value to others. You have resources and opportunities that no one else has. You have intrinsic value simply because you are a human being. You need to own these things.

Even if you do everything right, there's no guarantee that others won't treat you wrong. People can decide they don't like you with no legitimate reason. You can't control that. Develop thick skin, and your critics won't bother you as much.

2. Do Not Accept Blame That Doesn't Belong to You

Bullies are always looking for someone to blame. Don't allow them to blame you for things you're not responsible for. If something is your fault, own up to it. If it's not, decline to take the blame.

3. Refuse to Be a Victim

One of the reasons some people allow themselves to be bullied is that they feel powerless to do anything about what's happening to them; they believe that they're victims. It's important for you not to allow yourself to think that way. If you know who you are and you take a proactive approach to life, you are less likely to feel like a victim. You can't do everything, but you can do some things. You can't prevent others from treating you poorly, but you can decide how you will respond.

How Would You Work with a Difficult Leader Who Always Plays It Safe?

Many people are afraid of change, of risk, of failure. They don't want to let go of the known because they fear the unknown. These people's fears and worries are often overblown. Many times they're not based in reality. Yet these worries stop them from being productive and successful just the same. If you have leaders who always play it safe, you may be able to help them. Try doing the following:

Put Yourself in Their Shoes

To put yourself into your leaders' shoes, ask yourself three questions:

- **Where have they been?** This relates to their experiences. What kinds of things have happened to them that may be causing them to be afraid of change?

- **What do they feel?** This relates to their emotions. Try to find out not only how they feel but how they process their emotions and deal with things like stress.

- **What do they want?** This relates to expectations. If you know what they want and help them get it, maybe you'll get what you want too.

If you want to understand your leaders and work *with* them, you must see things from their perspective. That's the best way to help them and yourself.

Acknowledge Their Feelings

Leaders who avoid risk do so generally because they do not have the confidence to believe in their own success. Don't dismiss those feelings of fear and inadequacy. Instead acknowledge them. And as far as you are able, help them to achieve small wins. This can help them build their confidence.

Help Them Take Action

Sometimes what people need are facts. They need to see the greater value of a specific change. Yes, all of us can be hurt. All of us can and at times will fail. But progress always takes risk. Help your leaders weigh the potential gains and losses of taking action against the potential gains and losses of not taking it. If you can take the worst, take the risk.

If Your Leader Has Poor Leadership Skills, How Can You Run the Organization in a Respectful Way?

Often people who work for bosses with poor leadership skills try to fight the situation. That's an approach that is not likely to work. Instead they need to try to help their bosses to succeed, because if *we* want to be successful, we must try to help others to succeed. We can't undermine our leaders and expect our team to be successful. And if they're smart, they will understand that they cannot make it without us. We need each other.

1. Understand Your Leader

When people have asked me about working for poor leaders, I often find that they don't really know those leaders. They are so preoccupied by what their leaders aren't doing right that they don't even try to find out who they are. That's a mistake. To help yourself, you need to help them. To help them, you need to know what they care about.

Ask Your Leader...

- **What is your heart?** These are the things your leader cares about. As far as it's within your power, provide them.

- **What is your hope?** These are the things your leader wants to do. As far as they align with your values, promote them.

- **What causes you hurt?** These are the things your leader wants to avoid. As far as you're able, protect your leader from them.

- **How can I help?** There are many things your leader wants to do but cannot do alone. Your task is to partner with them to get those things done.

As you get to know your leaders and endeavor to help them, you will start to look at them as people first and leaders second. Your communication with them will improve. So will your connection. You may even begin to enjoy working together. And when we contribute to the success of our bosses, they are put in a position to rise. As they do, guess whom they want to bring along with them? The people who help them win.

2. Understand Your Support Role

Although your leadership skills may be greater than those of the people you work for, if you want to be successful, you have to play your part. You've been hired to play a supporting role. Do your best to fulfill it with excellence.

3. Bloom Where You're Planted

Few things impress leaders, whether they are strong or weak, like a worker who is both a starter and a finisher. If you have initiative and are a self-starter doing your work with joy, everyone will want to work with you. If you follow through on tasks and commitments, people will give you greater and greater responsibilities. The measure of a person is not what he or she says in the staff meeting, but rather what he or she does when the meeting is over.

4. Rise Above Others with a Right Attitude

It's hard for most people who work for weak leaders to maintain a great attitude. If you can be positive and supportive while all those around you are negative or complain, you will stand out and people will be drawn to you. Remember, good employees aren't people with a certain set of circumstances; they are people with a certain set of attitudes.

5. Succeed on Their Terms

When you're working in the middle of an organization with leaders above you, your success usually takes place on someone else's terms. You are not in charge of the definition of success. You cannot rewrite the rules of the game. The pathway to success has been set by others. The only thing you can do is succeed on the terms of others. This idea may frustrate you, but the reality is that everyone is accountable to someone and must succeed on others' terms.

In the end, the only thing you can do is lead your life. If you don't, others will, by determining what will happen to you. Life's greatest rewards come from your inner self, from the choices you make, from how you decide to live under whatever circumstances you find yourself in.

6

How to Navigate Leadership Transitions

Life means transition. Most people intuitively understand that the world is moving fast, yet they still have a difficult time with it. If you don't learn how to make good transitions, you either get run over or get left behind. One of the characteristics of good leaders is their ability to navigate transitions. That has always been true. They are able to make smooth transitions themselves. And they are also able to help their team members and their organizations do the same. The questions in this chapter will help you to become better at facing—and winning through—transition.

When Is the Right Time for a Successful Leader to Move On to a New Position?

Leaders often get restless. When they do, they start exploring opportunities and new mountains to climb. The more entrepreneurial the leaders, the shorter their attention spans often are. The key to knowing whether it's time to transition is recognizing that there are two kinds of restlessness: good and bad.

Good restlessness is healthy. It pulls you forward toward improvement. It comes from your desire to grow, to make a greater impact, to serve others more effectively.

Bad restlessness comes from being bored or unhappy. It comes from a desire to escape. It causes you to be impatient. You often jump out of where you are, but not *to* anything specific. And as a result, it can actually put you in a worse place. People experiencing the positive kind of restlessness are willing to hold steady until there's an opportunity to move to something better.

Ask yourself whether you have given the best you have where you are now. Don't move anywhere else until you have. Don't seek a move just to make things easier on yourself. To transition with integrity, you need to have done your best work possible. Then you can leave with a clear heart and mind. Besides, you always want to leave on a high note. You can see farther if you're at a peak than if you're in a valley.

Once you're certain that your desire to transition is motivated by the right reasons, use the following steps to help you move through the process the right way.

1. Consider Your Possibilities

Every transition in life is a trade-off. When you leave a negative place, you leave behind some good things. If you go to a great place, there will be some things about it that you won't like. It's not black and white. And the more successful you are, the harder it is to make trade-offs, because you give up more when you trade off and transition. That's why some people become successful and then become flat.

Patience and maturity will empower you to consider your possibilities as you seek to transition. During that time, study, reflect, pray, plan, read, and write. Look for opportunities. Interview people who are ahead of you in the journey. Use the time to your advantage.

2. Weigh the Risks and Rewards

If you are patient and keep your eyes open, you will find an opportunity. Before you make a transition, it is wise to do a risk assessment. Make lists of risks and rewards. It's not just a matter of which list is longer. Not all entries are equal. A single risk or reward may carry so much weight that it tips the balance.

As you weigh the risks against the rewards, be sure to take into account things that tap into your passion, giving them extra weight. And ask yourself these questions:

- **Are the potential rewards greater than the risks?**
  You don't want to take a giant leap for a small reward
  or risk a lot for the potential of a small gain.

- **Is what you hope to do achievable?** You may not be
  certain about your ability to achieve what you desire.
  But you must know it's *possible* to achieve it.

- **Can you recover from the downside?** It's OK to fail.
  It's not smart to fail in a way you can't recover from.

It's generally not wise to transition without having
clarity about where you want to go. You can follow your
instinct, but you don't want to do it uninformed.

3. Receive Affirmation from Your Inner Circle

The most important person you need affirmation from
when making a transition decision is yourself. You need to
know your own heart. You need to have confidence. You
don't want to make a move if you can't find peace within
yourself. Otherwise you'll be plagued by doubt if something goes wrong. And that makes it hard for you to keep
steady and persevere.

Having said that, it's wise for you to get input from the
people closest to you and from wise people ahead of you.
The right people's opinions, thoughts, perspectives, and
experience can provide a tremendous amount of clarity.
They can help you see the bigger picture, especially when

your head has been deep into the details. If your decision is right, their input should make that clearer to you.

4. Take Action and Move Forward

If you believe the decision to transition is right and you know where you desire to go, you need to take action. Most decisions people regret in life are the ones they make that lead to inaction. If you're getting older, the only thing worse than not having made a decision when you were younger is not making it now if you still can. Don't live your life haunted by the question "What if?"

When I'm in the right place doing the right thing, I don't think of any other possibilities. I just love what I'm doing and can't imagine doing anything else. I'm excited and I want everyone around me to be excited. When I start to feel some dissatisfaction, it's often because I can't grow any more and my current situation is limiting my potential. That's when I start to open myself up to other possibilities.

How Can a Leader Implement the Changes That an Organization Needs to Be Successful but Resists Making?

All change does not represent progress, but without change there can be no progress. And it is often up to leaders to initiate and implement changes. But here's the good news: if people need change, they often look to leaders for inspiration and guidance. If you find yourself in a position where you are the leader who must lead the charge for change, keep in mind the following guidelines:

Change What Needs to Be Changed, Not What Is Easy to Change

When organizations are having difficulties, leaders instinctively know that changes need to be made. One question is whether they will make real needed changes or merely cosmetic ones. Cosmetic changes are relatively easy to make. They give the semblance of change, but often don't actually produce positive results.

Changes that can make a difference are harder. Changing organizational culture when it's unhealthy, for example, is difficult. So is changing values. Or leaders and the way they are developed. But these kinds of efforts are what really change an organization.

Let Go of Yesterday So You Can Go to Tomorrow

If you are going to lead change, you need to clear out the old and outdated ways of thinking, and you need to help the people you lead to do the same. That's often not just a practical or intellectual exercise; it's also an emotional one. Acknowledge the importance of the past. Honor the people who have made past contributions. But also show them why they can't stay where they are, and why the place you want to take them is so much better.

Communicate the Message with Simplicity and Power

Good leaders take the complex and make it simple. That is a hallmark of a good communicator. That's not easy, but who ever said leadership was supposed to be easy? As you communicate the vision for change, give people multiple reasons for it. The more reasons for change, the more likely people are to accept it. Certainly the main reason will probably be that it is better for the organization. But how is it also good for customers, clients, and the community? And how is it better for the people in the organization who must implement the change? Never underestimate the importance of answering the question "What's in it for me?"

Activate Belief in People

As you work to implement changes, you must believe in them. Without conviction you won't give yourself 100 percent to the changes. People will sense that and will not follow you. But believing in the cause is not enough. You must also believe in the people who will make the change. Without that conviction they will not move forward. You energize an organization by energizing its people. You activate their belief in themselves. Your confidence in them will give them confidence in themselves.

Remove Barriers for People

Once you communicate the need and vision for change and help people to believe they *can* change, your most important task as a leader is to start removing barriers that will keep people from executing the plan. Barriers are usually created by outdated systems, complicated procedures, difficult people, or strained resources. To find the barriers, get out among the people, watch what they're doing, and listen to their complaints.

Lead with Speed

Speed is important in creating short-term wins. Never underestimate the significance of early victories for giving people confidence to keep moving forward. Wins nourish faith in the change effort. They give an emotional lift to the people who are carrying and implementing the change. And they silence critics. Every win helps to build momentum, which is a leader's best friend.

How Do I Change My Mind-Set from That of a Producer to That of a Leader?

Most of us get our first opportunity to lead because we are personally successful. We produce for the organization, and some leader in the organization wants us to help others do the same. When that happens, a person must make the mind shift from *me* to *we*.

If you're a good producer, you probably know how you personally contribute to the vision of the organization. Ask yourself, "How does this team contribute to the vision?" and "How can every individual member contribute to the team?" Your job is to maximize the team's effort to fulfill the vision.

You also need to work to build relationships with the people on your team. If you are naturally a task-oriented person, this may be a stretch. Get to know your team as individuals and try to connect with them. Look for ways to add value to them. Find ways to lift them up with encouragement and gratitude. You can't really know what everyone's best contribution is until you know everyone. As a producer, you already know how to win. As a leader, your job is to help the entire team win.

As an Entrepreneurial Leader of a Fast-Growing Organization, How Do I Know Whether to Transition My Role to Create Structure and Stability, or to Hire Leaders to Fulfill the New Needs?

It's obvious that in an organization that's not succeeding, leaders need to create change to get forward progress and create momentum. However, when organizations are highly successful, especially smaller organizations, leaders must make changes to sustain success and increase momentum. If they rely too long on past successes and keep doing what they've always done, the organization will eventually hit a wall.

In small entrepreneurial organizations, the top leaders are often the catalysts for the organization. They are the ones who see opportunities, produce organizational energy, and create synergy between the organization and its customers. If you are the catalyst for your organization, do not lose your strength. In small organizations, the leader's passion drives everything. So don't institutionalize your organization too quickly. Instead of changing your role, channel your energy. Here's how:

Invite Your Inner Circle to Help You Focus Your Energy

Most entrepreneurial leaders don't struggle to find opportunities. They struggle to focus on the best opportunities. And the more gifted the leaders, the greater the number of options available to them.

One way to find your focus is to form a committee that will regularly review opportunities, discuss strategy, and weigh choices. Choose people who will share their perspectives, offer wisdom, and remind you to stay in your strength zone even when you step out of your comfort zone. They need to understand the importance of your entrepreneurial spirit and have the wisdom and skill to channel it, not control it or try to stop it for their own comfort or convenience.

Meet fairly frequently—at least monthly. This is not a one-and-done kind of activity, especially in an entrepreneurial organization, where the landscape is constantly changing and you're continually reevaluating your opportunities.

Enlist People Who Maximize and Magnify Your Energy

Once you've narrowed your focus to the things that have the greatest potential, you need to make the most of them. One of the things I've always looked for in people on my team is the ability to maximize the opportunities we have.

Every experience that involves other people can be magnified by those who understand the value of an opportunity, the importance of timing, the quality of the experience, and the impact of numbers. If you're the one who sees and seizes opportunities, bring around yourself leaders and support staff who can make the most of those opportunities.

Empower People Who Have Skill and Energy in Areas Where You Lack Them

I'm not big on structure. I think too many organizations overemphasize it. And I think a lot of organizations use reorganization to try to solve problems when they don't know what else to do. Instead I prefer a leadership-driven model of organization. Put the right leaders into place, train and develop them well, then empower them to make an impact in their area.

As your organization grows, look for people who share your values and have a deep appreciation for opportunity and impact, but who can bring organizational skills to the table to help you build a framework that will further growth and serve the vision. The energy that you bring and that is already felt throughout the company will be even better when it's channeled correctly.

What Leadership Principles Enable a Failed Leader to Lead Again Successfully?

When leaders fail, whether the breakdown occurs as a result of poor character, bad judgment, or lack of skill, one of the first things they think about is often how to move back into leadership. I think that's only natural, because leaders love to lead. However, if they don't first stop and take time to correct whatever problems they've had, they are very likely to keep repeating the same mistakes.

If you've failed as a leader and lost your position, you need to consider the following before attempting to return to leadership:

Evaluation: What Went Wrong?

Before you can move back into a leadership role, you need to fix whatever problems you have in your leadership. You can't do that if you don't know what they are. Where did you go wrong? Was it a mistake in strategy? Did you lack skills necessary for good leadership? Do your problems stem from poor self-leadership? The last is the most common issue for failed leaders, but it is often the most difficult for them to see on their own. If you're not sure what went wrong, talk to people with firsthand knowledge to get their perspective.

Emotional Strength: Can You Bounce Back?

I strongly believe that people need to learn how to fail forward, and I believe they can. However, it requires emotional strength. If you've failed, you need to be able to face your failure, own up to it, and process it emotionally. And you also need to regain your footing and rebuild your emotional strength and resilience before you try to lead others again. If you haven't regained that emotional strength, you're likely to repeat the same mistakes, especially if character and self-leadership issues were at the root of your past problems.

Evolution: Can You Make the Adjustments Needed for Future Success?

After you've identified what went wrong and regathered your strength emotionally, you still have a lot of internal work to do. Maybe you need to put yourself on a personal growth plan whereby you read a dozen books and attend some conferences. Maybe you need to seek counseling to help you with character issues. Maybe you need to find a mentor. Maybe you need to further your education. Maybe you need greater accountability. You need to figure it out and make necessary adjustments. If you're not willing and able to do that, you probably should not step back into leadership.

Once you're done working on yourself, you still need to do a lot of work with others. You need to earn respect and rebuild trust with people. The process of building trust begins with being honest and transparent about your weaknesses, frailties, and mistakes. People don't expect their leaders to be perfect, but they do expect them to be honest. If you understand your humanness, can learn to accept it, and are open about it, you're in a position to ask people's forgiveness. That's where the trust-building process starts. Many people will never trust you until you ask forgiveness. Some won't trust you even then, but if you're honest and humble about your failure, ask forgiveness, try to make amends, and demonstrate a willingness to change, you've done what you can to move forward. You have no control over whether others forgive you or trust you again. You can only do everything in your power to earn trust from the people you work with. Just be sure that if you regain their trust, you move forward with integrity and don't willingly violate it again.

Why Do Some Leaders Fail to Have a Successor?

Some leaders simply fail to plan for succession. They don't like contemplating the end of the leadership road for themselves, so they simply refuse to think about it. They act as though they will live and lead forever, and they either die while still holding on to their positions or get pushed out once they are no longer effective.

But often when organizations fail to have a successor, it's not because the leader doesn't want one. It's because one of the following happens:

- **The organization doesn't accept the new leader.** Sometimes the people in an organization are so entrenched in old thinking that they won't allow a new person to lead them.

- **The new leader doesn't like the organization.** Sometimes there isn't a good fit, and it's not discovered until the new leader takes the reins.

- **The new leader doesn't fit the corporate culture.** If the vision and values of the leader don't match up with those of the organization, there will be a clash.

- **The new leader fails to bring about successful changes.** Sometimes the person chosen to succeed a leader isn't as good as hoped due to lack of ability, capacity, experience, knowledge, or relational connection.

- **The old guard sabotages the efforts of the new leader.** Any time an organization contains leaders who believe they were passed over in favor of another leader, there is the danger that they may do what they can to make the new leader fail.

- **The old leader sabotages the efforts of the new leader.** Occasionally the person stepping down has a hard time seeing someone else succeed in the position.

There are certainly no guarantees when it comes to succession, yet I believe it is something worth fighting for. The

Law of Legacy in *The 21 Irrefutable Laws of Leadership* states, "A leader's lasting value is measured by succession."

What Are the Most Important Things a Leader Transitioning Out of a Position Can Do to Ensure the Success of the Person Taking Over the Role?

If you are thinking about succession, whether because of a transition to another organization or because you believe your time to lead is coming to an end, that needs to be your primary focus as a leader. I believe you, your organization, and your successor will benefit if you proceed in this way:

1. Plan Ahead

As the outgoing leader, you must do your best to prepare yourself, your successor, and your organization for the upcoming transition. It is your responsibility to the people you lead to make the change as smooth as possible.

2. Pick Your Successor

In some organizations you don't get to pick your successor. It's done by another leader or by a board of directors. However, if it is within your power, pick someone who has the potential to take the organization further than you have. Obviously you want to look for high leadership gifting and strong skills for your industry. But also keep in mind how long the person will have the potential to lead.

Planning for Succession

1. **Prepare yourself.** Many leaders have a hard time letting go of their leadership positions. Some can't handle it emotionally. Some have not prepared financially. Others have not discussed it with their families. Get yourself ready for the idea.

2. **Look for several potential successors.** If you are in a position to pick your successor, look for several people with the potential to replace you. Ideally you would have a pool of people to pick from.

3. **Let the organization know change is on the horizon.** Transitions from one leader to another can be traumatic. Don't spring it on your people. Let them know in plenty of time, if it's within your power.

You probably naturally gravitate to people in your own age bracket. Birds of a feather flock together. If you're nearing retirement age, don't allow yourself to think of successors of your own generation. Reach down. Look for young leaders with potential. They may not have as much seasoning and experience, but they give the organization a better chance to succeed in the long run.

3. Prepare Your Successor

Focus your efforts on giving the upcoming successor every possible opportunity to take on responsibility, make decisions, and influence the organization *before* the transition. Your goal as a leader should be to work yourself out of a job. Develop your successor as a person and leader. Don't think solely in terms of the job. Try to reproduce yourself. Equip and empower your successor to the point that they can do the job as well as you—and then some. If you give all you can and add it to all they are and bring to the table, you give the person and the organization a good chance to succeed.

4. Take Care of Any Unfinished Business

If you are leaving an organization on a high note, you probably have a clear perspective on your organization. That means you know where the problems are. No one is in a better position to take care of unfinished business than you are. You have people's respect, and you have the power to solve difficulties for your successor. So why not do that? You can afford to take hits because you have so much credibility. You can create space for your successor to move forward without those difficulties. What a fantastic gift.

5. Say Goodbye

When it's time for you to resign, leave. Few things are more debilitating to a new leader than having his predecessor meddling in the organization and undermining his leadership. So when you step down from the leadership of your organization, get out of the way. Let your successor do the job outside of your shadow.

6. Make Yourself Available to Your Successor

Part of saying goodbye is not offering unsolicited advice. However, your successor will appreciate it if you make yourself available when and if they choose to reach out to you. There are things only you can know. You have a perspective that is unique and valuable. Offer it when asked.

How Do You Handle Leaving Great People Who Came to a Company Because You Asked Them to?

Telling people goodbye can be difficult. When you make a transition, no matter how necessary it is or how well you do it, you will disappoint people you care about. You should not allow that to stop you if it's the right thing to do. Help the people you can. Set your successor up for success. And leave with integrity. You can't expect yourself to do more than that.

What Should Be the Legacy of a Successful Leader?

Legacies that matter are connected with people. A hundred years from now, all that will matter is the people that you connected with in such a way that you added value and meaning to their lives. There are people in your world who would be thrilled to learn from you—not just the person who will succeed you in your leadership position, but people in every area of your life.

Achievement comes to people who are able to do great things for themselves. Success comes when they lead followers to do great things for them. But a legacy is created only when leaders put their people into a position to do great things without them. The legacy of successful leaders lives on through the people they touch along the way. The only things you can change permanently are the hearts of the people you lead.

7

How to Develop Leaders

Everything rises and falls on leadership. If you want to maximize your potential and make a difference, you must become a better leader. If you want to make an impact on your world, you must help others to become better leaders. Leaders are hard to find, hard to train, and hard to hold. They want to go their own way. But developing leaders is perhaps the most rewarding activity you will ever engage in during your lifetime.

What Is the Best Way to Identify Leadership Potential in Others?

Your success is more dependent on your ability to find and attract good people than on anything else. You will develop good leaders only if you find people who have strong leadership potential. That becomes much easier if you know what you're looking for.

I've been developing leaders for nearly forty years. I want to share my list of criteria with you so that you too will be able to spot people with leadership potential, recruit them to your team, and begin developing them.

1. Leaders Are Catalysts

Every leader I've ever known has had the ability to make things happen. This is often how they first become recognized. When I see someone who can make things happen, it grabs my attention. The ability to make things happen doesn't automatically make a person a leader, but I've yet to meet a leader who didn't have the ability to make things happen.

2. Leaders Are Influencers

Leadership is influence, so of course potential leaders must have the ability to influence other people. Influence is something that cannot be delegated. Every person who wants to lead must possess it, at least to some degree.

As you look at potential leaders and try to gauge their level of leadership, pay attention to whom they influence. Do they influence only their friends and family? That's a pretty low level of influence. If other workers in their department or on their team are influenced, that shows a greater level of ability. When workers outside their department or team follow, that shows even greater promise. If their colleagues follow them, they've developed a pretty high degree of influence. And if they influence you and other people higher than they are in leadership, it indicates quite a bit of ability. These people are already leading and have great promise.

3. Leaders Are Relationship Builders

One thing that holds many talented and intelligent people back from being good leaders is a lack of people skills. Someone with weak people skills can become a reasonably good manager, because management is focused on systems and procedures. But nobody without good people skills can be a great leader.

When people on the team don't like someone, they will often try to hurt that person. If they can't cause harm, they will simply refuse to help. If they have no real choice and are *required* to help, they will still be mentally and emotionally against the individual and will hope he or she doesn't succeed. And even if the person does manage to succeed, the victories he or she achieves can feel very hollow and be short-lived. Elevating someone with bad people skills is a recipe for failure.

Good leaders like people and people like them. They work at connecting with others and they continually look for opportunities to connect.

4. Leaders Are Gatherers

Potential leaders have a quality about them whereby they are always "holding court." Other people are attracted to them.

They want to hear what they say. They like being around them because exciting things happen. Often these people are funny and entertaining. They just seem to possess the quality of attraction. People like spending time with them.

When leaders speak, people listen. In a meeting, people often wait to hear what leaders have to say. When outgoing people *without* leadership potential speak, nobody listens. They're merely making a speech without an audience. They find it hard to gather people and grab their attention. Whenever I see a person who continually gathers a crowd, I pay attention, because I want to assess whether that person has other qualities that signify leadership potential.

5. Leaders Are Value Adders

All good leaders add value. They see their role as leader as a means to help others, not just themselves. Can someone lead others without adding value? Certainly. The world is filled with leaders who push others down to raise themselves up, who lead for the power and perks. But their leadership is fleeting. It adds no value to others. And its impact on the world is negative. Who wants that kind of person on their team?

6. Leaders Are Opportunists

Good leaders see and seize opportunities. They are continually on the lookout for ways to help their organization and advance their team. Leaders, by definition, are out front.

They take new territory and others follow them. Great leaders don't merely send others out. They lead the charge. They see opportunities, prepare to move forward, and then say, "Follow me." When you see someone who is able to see opportunities and is willing to take good risks, pay attention. You may be looking at a leader.

7. Leaders Are Finishers

Leaders don't make excuses. They take responsibility, embrace opportunity, and follow through. They live up to their commitments and they can be counted on to finish. They commit and follow through.

Who Are Your Leaders?

Spend some time looking at the people in your sphere of influence. Have you identified the potential leaders? Whose name would get a check mark for each of the following leadership characteristics?

Catalyst

Influencer

Relationship builder

Gatherer

Value adder

Opportunist

Finisher

Few things are harder than trying to help people without leadership potential to lead. However, when you pick the right people, developing them is a pleasure.

Is Developing Leaders More Art or Science?

Some people want to develop leaders through a highly structured and inflexible system, to try to produce them the way manufacturers punch shapes out of sheets of metal. Other people want the development of their leaders to be entirely organic and without planning, every lesson growing out of the situation at hand. But the truth is that leadership development is both science and art.

ART	SCIENCE
Based on Intuition	Rooted in Fact
Recognizing Talent	Sharpening Talent Through Practice
Inspiring Performance	Evaluating Performance
Developing Relationships	Developing Skills
Identifying Teachable Moments	Implementing a Training Method
Knowing When to Move	Preparing Before the Move

Daniel Goleman has done a lot to help people understand the intuitive side of leadership. His research and writing on emotional intelligence shows that while the qualities traditionally associated with leadership—such as intelligence, technical skills, and determination—are required for success, they tell only part of the story. Effective leaders also possess emotional intelligence, which includes self-awareness, intuition, a capacity for self-leadership, empathy, and people skills. These "softer" skills represent the more creative side of leadership and must be developed as much as the hard skills. As you develop leaders, you must identify, nurture, and develop both skill sets.

How Do You Help People Realize the Talent Within Them? How Do You Help People Believe in Themselves?

Leaders help people to believe in the vision and in their leadership. But they also help people to believe in themselves. They help people turn hope into action. Perhaps the most rewarding aspect of leadership is seeing people with hope believe in themselves, develop themselves, and blossom into effective leaders. If you desire to help your people do that, proceed in this way:

Find Evidence That They Want to Grow

You cannot get someone who does not want to grow to embrace personal growth. People must ultimately make that decision for themselves. How can you tell who wants to grow? Attitude and effort. People worthy of your time and attention have a learning attitude. They're open to instruction and hungry to grow. They may not yet be convinced that they can reach what you recognize as their potential, but they have the desire. And they are already making an effort to grow. Their efforts may not be strategic. They may not be focused. They may not even be effective. But you can see a spark there. That's all you need to get started.

Identify Their Strengths

The number one problem of people who want to grow but aren't reaching their potential is that they major in their weaknesses. That's what they've been taught to do for most of their lives. Think about when you got your report card when you were a child. If you got an A in math and a C-minus in reading, what did your teacher say you needed to work on? Your reading.

However, that's not a good strategy as you get older. If you want to be successful, you need to build on your strengths, not shore up your weaknesses. Nobody pays for average. Nobody purposely hires mediocrity. People pay for excellence. If you're above average at something, you have a shot at becoming excellent at it.

The people you lead may not know what they're good at. Many people grow up with little or no encouragement from the significant adults in their lives. Many people take a convenient job and never give thought to what they could be great at. As a leader you need to help people figure out where they have potential and should grow.

Increase Their Confidence

There are two kinds of people who have confidence: those with a high level of mastery in their area of strength and those who have no knowledge whatsoever and think everything's easy because they've never done anything. Then there's a middle group, which is the largest. These people need your help gaining confidence in themselves.

As people start trying to grow and tackle new challenges, they usually become insecure. Trying to conquer new territory can be scary. That's why you need to lend them your belief. Tell them, "I understand that you're on a journey. This is foreign to you. You may be a bit nervous. That's OK. I believe in you. It's going to be all right. You may not get this on the first try, but you're going to get it. You're a winner and you're going to win. Keep at it."

When you express belief in people, it goes right to their souls. It gives them hope. It stirs their sense of purpose. It helps them be someone they've never been before and do things they've never done before. Knowing that you believe in them causes them to rise up.

Give Them a Place to Practice

Training is good. Mentoring is fantastic. Development is incredible. But if you don't give emerging leaders a place to practice, their knowledge will never become practical experience. Leadership is so complex that you can't learn it just from a book. You can get ideas. You can open doors mentally. You can understand skill sets, but you won't acquire them and grow if you don't put them into action. People need to make mistakes and learn from them. They need to find out what works for them. They need to work with real people who have strengths and weaknesses, problems and quirks.

Coach Them to Improvement

As people try practicing new skills, you need to allow them to fail safely. People always learn more from their failures than they do from their successes. Walk alongside them to give them security and to help them through the most difficult problems. Share with them where they made mistakes and how they can overcome them. Tell them what to work on. And encourage them to keep trying. When you first begin to coach them, you may be fairly hands-on. You may stay close to them. As they gain experience, give them more space.

Keep Increasing Their Responsibilities

At this point many leaders make a mistake. As soon as the emerging leader gains a degree of self-sufficiency, they leave that leader alone, grateful that they can finally carry their own weight. It's a relief to have someone who can share the load. But don't stop there. If you have developed a leader who can be successful independently, you will have done more than most other leaders do. And it might feel like you're done. But for the best developers of people, that's not enough. If you continue to work with new leaders and keep increasing their level of responsibility, they will continue to grow and improve.

Your goal should always be to work yourself out of a job. Keep giving your leaders more and more weight to carry. Allow them to benefit from your experience until they are capable of doing your job. That takes security on your part. But if you do that, when it comes time for *you* to move up to greater responsibility or move on to a new challenge, you will have people who can step in and take your place. That should always be your goal as a leader.

How Can You Help People to Achieve Their Maximum Potential When They Won't Leave Their Comfort Zone?

Many people don't have a greater vision for their lives. And it's easy for people, even those who want to grow, to get into a rut and stay in their comfort zone. As a leader you should try to encourage them to move forward and reach for their potential. You're not responsible for their response. Every individual has to take responsibility for that. But you can model growth, encourage them, and try to be a catalyst for positive change. Here's how:

Show Them a Vision for Their Better Future

If people cannot see a better future for themselves, you need to show it to them. Start by asking them questions: If you could be anything you wanted, what would you be? If you could do anything you wanted, what would you do? If you knew you could not fail, what would you try? See what stirs inside them. Many people have dreams deep inside that need only a bit of encouragement to coax out.

Treat Them Not as They Are, but as They Could Be

If you were to treat the people around you as they could be instead of as they are, how do you think they would respond? If they've been in a rut a long time, they might not rise up right away. You might have to keep speaking positively about them and treating them as people who desire to reach their potential, but I believe that in time most would rise up. And if they don't, what have you lost? Nothing. Give it a try. Speak positively about a better future for them, and they just might try to live up to it.

Set Them Up for a Win

Many times, people aren't willing to leave their comfort zone because they are convinced that they cannot win. You can change that by setting them up for success. If you put them in a position where an easy win is almost guaranteed, they can have that winning experience inspire them to move forward.

How Do You Determine How Much Time to Give Someone You're Developing?

Everybody in your organization needs time and assistance, but that doesn't mean you can help everybody personally.

You should be kind and supportive of everyone, but you must pick and choose whom you will develop. If you focus on the top 20 percent of your team, the people with the highest skills and greatest potential to grow, you can ask them to help support and develop the remaining 80 percent.

How to Identify Your Top 20 Percent

Here's what to look for when determining who might be in your top 20 percent:

- **Passion:** Are they excited? Are they positive about the team? Does the vision energize them? Is the work they do fulfilling to them? You don't want to be required to push someone to be developed.

- **Teachability:** Are they growing now? Are they open to new ideas? Are they humble and willing to learn? You want to invest in people who are hungry.

- **Capacity:** What is their potential? Is there plenty of room for growth? Do they possess talent in the area in which you want to develop them? How far could they go if you were to help them?

You may have lots of people worth investing in. If so, don't try to develop more than the top 20 percent. If you spread yourself too thin, people won't get your best. On the other hand, if you judge that you have only one person with potential, invest in him or her.

Once you've identified whom you want to develop, ask them how much time *they* think they need in order to be successful. I think we don't ask these kinds of questions enough. Most of the time, good people will be strategic in their response. Not everyone will be, but good people usually are, because they don't want to just hang out. They want to get things done. They want to achieve something.

If the amount of time they request is appropriate—based on their potential and the amount of time you have—give it to them, but make it convenient to you. Ask them to fit into your schedule and travel to you. And when you do get together, make the most of that time. Make it count.

When Do You Release or "Give Up" on People You Are Leading, After You've Done What You Can to Help Them Grow?

Many leaders find it difficult to know when to stop investing in someone they once believed in. Some leaders give up too soon. Others hang on to someone way too long, hoping that person will get back on track. I believe it's OK to release people if one of these things happens:

You've Given Them the Chance to Change but They Haven't

If you've made it clear to them *how* they need to change, you've explained *why* they need to change, and you've given them all the resources that make it *possible* for them to change, yet they still do not change, you need to stop investing in them. If a person only ever wants to talk about the problem, but not actually do anything about it, he or she may care only about being heard and understood rather than about changing and growing. If the person decides not to follow your direction, you can choose not to give him or her any more of your time. Why invest in someone who doesn't want to follow your direction and grow?

They Have Broken Trust

When people you're investing in break trust with you, it's time to stop giving them your time and energy. It's been said that if you can't trust everything a person says, you can't trust anything they say. If someone isn't trustworthy anymore, they've violated the relationship. There's no good way to move forward.

You Realize You Would Not Hire Them Again Today

Sometimes you realize that people don't have the potential you thought you saw in them when you hired them. Maybe you believed in them more than they believe in themselves, they were in an unusually good season when you met them, or you were mistaken about the talent and skills you thought you saw. No matter which of these things might be true, you may have come to realize that if you were hiring someone today to fill their role, you would not pick them. If that's true, it's time to stop investing in them. You can't make people into something they're not. It's time to move on and give your time and energy to someone else who can help the team.

I Have Empowered Others to Lead and Come Back Only to Find Them Without Progress and Back to Doing Things the Old Way. What Should I Do Differently?

People have to change themselves through their choices. The only thing you can do is create a positive environment that encourages growth and change. If there are people in your organization or on your team who aren't learning, growing, and changing, and you've not yet created an environment that promotes growth, try doing the following:

Treat High Achievers as Partners Rather than Employees

One of the most positive things you can do for your high achievers is close the gap between them and you. Treat your top talent as partners. Your working relationship should look more like a strategic alliance than like a traditional employment arrangement. That means that as the leader, you're not withholding information from your team to maintain an advantage. You're asking for advice. You're listening as much as or more than you're talking. You include your team in the formation of the vision. You share decision making. You work together with them in everything, rather than handing down assignments.

If you do this consistently, you will see exponential

growth in your best people, because they will learn how you think. You will also find that people start carrying the weight of responsibility and volunteer to take on challenges rather than having them assigned to them.

Stay Ahead of Your Strongest Players

You cannot set the tone for the environment if you don't stay ahead of your strongest team members. This doesn't mean that you have to know everything or that you have to lead the pack in every category. I have many people on my team who know more than I do in certain areas. But when it comes to leadership, I work to remain the strongest on the team. As leaders creating a positive environment for growth, we must continue to grow, read, research, and interact with other organizations and leaders to remain on the cutting edge. If we do that, we will be able to model creative thinking, emotional security, and servant leadership for others.

Reward Achievers Financially

I've found that the best people in my organization have already made the transition from seeking success to striving for significance. They are working for fulfillment, not finances. However, I have always made it a point to reward my top talent financially as a statement of my appreciation. I never want finances to be a distraction or a thorn in my people's side. If they're paid well, they can focus on the things that really matter.

Invest in Achievers Relationally

Mentor your best people. Give them time one-on-one. Give them access to you and build a developmental relationship. Your most talented people have a strong desire to learn and grow. Feed that desire. And encourage them to engage in this same process with people who are behind them and coming up.

Stretch High Achievers Continually

A sure sign that someone is a high achiever is that they want to be challenged. That's always true of top talent. If you have exceptional people on your team, you need to be continually thinking of ways to challenge them. Don't allow them to get bored, because if they do, they'll get restless and start looking for other opportunities.

Give people your best, but don't carry the weight of their choices. Don't carry the weight of the results. Help whom you can, and allow the others to find another environment or another leader who can help them.

How Can We Overcome Disappointment When We Invest Ourselves in Our Upcoming Leaders and They Leave?

To be honest, you don't get over it. The best you can do is try to gain wisdom from it. Loss is the beginning of wisdom. The pain and hurt of having great people leave you makes you give greater attention to the process, especially if you have invested heavily in the people who leave. Try to wish them well, and don't allow yourself to get bitter.

You may be tempted to stop investing in people as a result. But the only thing worse than developing people and losing them is not developing them and keeping them. If you stop developing people, your organization will decline while other organizations pass you by. The best thing you can do is learn from your experiences and do your best to hold on to your strongest people going forward.

We are living and leading in a world of free agents. People leave for a variety of reasons. You may or may not be able to keep all your best people. They may leave for reasons that have nothing to do with you. But do your best to keep them. Don't give them reasons to leave. Make your purpose larger than you. Give them every opportunity to work for significance, not just success. Pay them as well as you can. Help them grow. And create a great environment that makes it very difficult for people to leave. That's all you can do.

What's the Most Important Thing a Leader Must Learn in Order to Be a Leader of Leaders?

There's only one way to lead leaders. Become a better leader yourself. Good leaders do not follow poor ones. People naturally follow leaders stronger than themselves. So if you want to be a leader of leaders, you will need to earn the right. You will need to achieve success first. The higher the capacity of the leaders you desire to lead, the bigger the success you need to have in your history. You'll need to keep raising your leadership capacity. You'll need to make growth a major goal and dedicate yourself to it. And you'll also have to keep your ego in check. If you have a compulsive need to be the alpha dog, the other top dogs won't want to work with you.

How Do You Move People into Your Inner Circle?

Most of the people who are in my inner circle have arrived there because they've proven themselves or because I saw where they could add value. Before I think about moving someone into my inner circle, I consider the following:

1. Time

I don't put someone into my inner circle without having history with that person. It's just too risky. You need to know someone's character before you allow them to handle important parts of your world. It also takes time to develop the relationship. I tend to make quick judgments about people. I'm also very trusting. So I have to fight the urge to bring someone in too quickly.

2. Trust

For your inner circle to be effective, you must totally trust the people in it. You can't be asking about their motives. If you do, you'll always keep up your guard, and they won't be able to help you the way they need to.

3. Experience

To be in my inner circle, people need to have experience—not just professional experience, but life experience. I believe people need seasoning to make good decisions. For that reason I don't want anyone too young. There's no one currently in my inner circle younger than his or her late thirties.

4. Success

For someone to be in my inner circle, they need to have achieved some success. They need to have proven themselves. They must possess the proven ability to add value to me and the organization. Being asked into the inner circle isn't their chance to "make it." They need to already have some wins in their résumé to be considered for the inner circle. You get in because you're good, not because you have the potential to be good.

5. Compatibility

Life is too short to work every day with people you don't like. There isn't anyone in my inner circle I'm not compatible with. The group has a variety of personality types and a variety of skills and gifting. But we're all on the same page and all get along great. Every day of my life I tell the people in my inner circle that I love them, and I really mean it.

6. Capacity

A person can bring every one of those other things to the table, but if they don't have capacity, they cannot be in my inner circle. I move fast, I get a lot done, and I expect the people on my team to do the same. Neither I nor the rest of the team has time to wait around for someone who's lagging behind. We need for people to keep up, not to be trying to help them catch up. We can work together only if we're all together.

Finding Your Inner Circle

What qualities will you require for people in your inner circle? Is your list the same as mine? Or do you require something different? Think about it. Then start building your own inner circle. Your goal should be to surround yourself with a small group of people who love you for who you are, possess the ability to add value to you, have a sense of loyalty to you, and desire to help you achieve your purpose. You, in return, need to help them achieve theirs.

If you have not yet developed an inner circle, I strongly encourage you to do so. Some members will eventually leave you. Some will probably hurt you. All of them will help you. And you will never regret bringing them together. When you're my age, you will look back at your time with them as one of your greatest joys.

Conclusion

If you approached this book with the desire to grow more as a leader, I hope I was able to help you. As you learn more about leadership and develop as a leader, you will probably find that there are always new ways to improve. I've been studying leadership for fifty years, and I'm still trying to learn and grow. I frequently still ask myself, "What do successful people know about leadership that I don't?" And whenever I do, I discover new insights that I can apply to my life.

As you move forward, remember that good leaders are learners. If you are always looking for ways to grow, and asking the right people the right questions, I believe you will become a better leader and mentor to other leaders.

A Special Thank-You

I would like to thank the hundreds of people who asked questions for this book and especially the following individuals whose great questions appear in the book. The answers given are only as good as the questions asked. If this book serves people well, it is because of the quality of your questions.

Farshad Asl*

Andrew Axon

Rudolf Bakkara

John Barrett*

Art Barter

Betsi Bixby*

David Cipura

Beckie Cisler

Brandon Cockrell

Mark Cole

Jose Cordova

Anthony Coyoy

John DeWalle

David Emmanuel

Andre Finley

Aaron Frizzelle

Arnulfo Jose Suarez Gaeke

Brittany Gardner

Suvasish Ghosh

George Gomes

Ralph Govea

Deja Green

Virginia Gronley*

Charles Grubb

Penny Guinnette

Dean Haberlock

Peter Harding

Nathan Hellman

Eric Herrick

David Igbanoi

Loh Jen-Li Jenline

Osia Jerry

Laura Lambert
Rick Lester*
Lynette Little
Trudy Menke*
Benedick Naceno
Lusanda Ncapayi
Cyril Okeke
Rick Olson
Jenny Pace
Marc Pope
Lister Rayner
Dan Reiland
D. Roberts
Lynsey Robinson
Monika Patricia Rohr
Diane Runge

Amine Sahel
Vanessa Sanchez*
Eileen Schwartz*
Israel Silva*
Barry Smith*
David Specht
Sarah Stanley
David Stone
Timothy Teasdale*
Elias Tona
Jason Viergutz
Mike Walt
Misty West
Jeff Williams
Dale Witherington
Fernando Zambrano*

* Denotes John Maxwell Team Coach

John Maxwell's Bestselling Successful People Series—Over 1 Million Copies Sold

HOW SUCCESSFUL PEOPLE THINK

Change Your Thinking, Change Your Life

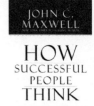

Good thinkers are always in demand. They solve problems, never lack ideas, and always have hope for a better future. In this compact read for today's fast-paced world, Maxwell reveals eleven types of successful thinking, and how you can maximize each to revolutionize your work and life.

HOW SUCCESSFUL PEOPLE LEAD

Taking Your Influence to the Next Level

True leadership is not generated by your title. In fact, being named to a position is the lowest of the five levels every effective leader achieves. But you can learn how to be more than a boss people are required to follow, and extend your influence beyond your immediate reach for the benefit of others.

HOW SUCCESSFUL PEOPLE GROW

15 Ways to Get Ahead in Life

John Maxwell explores the principles that are proven to be the most effective catalysts for personal growth. You can learn what it takes to strengthen your self-awareness, broaden your prospects, and motivate others with your positive influence.

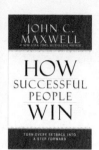

HOW SUCCESSFUL PEOPLE WIN

Turn Every Setback into a Step Forward

No one wins at everything. But with this book John Maxwell will help you identify the invaluable life lessons that can be drawn from disappointing outcomes and turn every loss into a gain.

MAKE TODAY COUNT

The Secret of Your Success Is Determined by Your Daily Agenda

How can you know if you're making the most of today so you can have a better tomorrow? By following the twelve daily disciplines Maxwell describes in this book to give maximum impact in minimum time.

A *Minute* with MAXWELL

Your Free Daily Video Coaching with John

John C. Maxwell's leadership principles are as timeless as they are true. His practical and purpose-driven approach to leadership drives him to live out what he teaches every day. Let John support your success by equipping you with leadership teachings to apply to your life.

Learn and grow every day…

Enjoy **FREE** wisdom & wit from world renown expert, John Maxwell, on how your success can rise and fall "with every word."

John will provide you the most **powerful video minute** of coaching on the planet.

Benefit from John's 40+ years as one of the world's top communicators **AT NO COST TO YOU!**

As a **BONUS**, send John your word, and he will teach on it during one of his videos.

IT'S FREE
Don't Wait!

Visit
www.JohnMaxwellTeam.com/LeadershipAnswers
and register today!

EQUIP®

PARTNERING WITH CHURCHES TO MOBILIZE BELIEVERS TO BE SALT & LIGHT IN THEIR COMMUNITIES

2050 Sugaloaf Circle
Duluth, GA 30097
678.225.3300
www.iequip.org